"A must read if you are considering buying a home."

—Leslie Nichols, Realtor, RE/MAX Professional Group

"This is a great how-to book for the real estate buyer. The author has first-hand experience as a realtor and has done her homework researching every step of the buying and financing process. Especially helpful for first time buyers."

—Teesie Howell, Senior Loan Officer, National City Mortgage.

Buying a House on a *Shoestring*

Find and Purchase the Home of Your Dreams Without Breaking the Bank

Piper Nichole

Author of *The For Sale By Owner Handbook*

CAREER PRESS

Franklin Lakes, NJ

BUYING A HOUSE ON A SHOESTRING
EDITED BY KATHRYN HENCHES
TYPESET BY MICHAEL FITZGIBBON
Cover design by Eric Ottinger
Printed in the U.S.A. by Book-mart Press

To order this title, please call toll-free 1-800-CAREER-1 (NJ and Canada: 201-848-0310) to order using VISA or MasterCard, or for further information on books from Career Press.

CAREER PRESS

The Career Press, Inc., 3 Tice Road, PO Box 687,
Franklin Lakes, NJ 07417
www.careerpress.com

Library of Congress Cataloging-in-Publication Data

Nichole, Piper, 1981-
Buying a house on a shoestring : find and purchase the home of your dreams without breaking the bank / by Piper Nichole.
p. cm.
Includes index.
ISBN-13: 978-156414-939-8
ISBN-10: 1-56414-939-0
1. House buying—United States—Handbooks, manuals, etc. I. Title.

HD259.N53 2007
643′.120973--dc22

2007004924

Dedication

With much love, this book is dedicated to Mom (thank you sooo much!), Devin, Nicholas, Sydney, Joel, and Dad.

Acknowledgments

I would genuinely like to say a *huge thank you* to the following folks for making this book possible: Mom (Thank you sooo much for all your support, *all the time* and staying up with me all those nights as I worked on this project! Hehehe!); Bob Diforio of D4EO Literary Agency (Thank you so much for making my dream come true!) and a special, special thank you to everyone at Career Press—Ron Fry, Michael Pye, Michael Lewis, Laurie Kelly-Pye, Adam Schwartz, Linda Reinecker, Kristen Parkes, Kathryn Henches, Michael Fitzgibbon, Diana Walsh, and everyone involved!

A gracious thank you to the experts that took the time to participate and share their excellent advice in *Buying a House on a Shoestring*: National Association of Realtors 2006 President Tom Stevens; Stephanie Singer; American Society of Home Inspectors 2006 president and owner of Shelterworks, Inc. in Dover, NJ, Joe Corsetto; Christiana Brenner of Manning Selvage & Lee (Chicago); National Association of Certified Home Inspectors founder Nick Gromicko; National City Mortgage Senior Loan Officer Teesie Howell; Quicken Loans CEO Bill Emerson and Mike Dunklee; Wells Fargo executive vice president and retail national sales manager Brad Blackwell, Jason D. Menke, and Kevin M. Waetke; Fair Isaac Company Craig Watts (MyFico.com); Experian Vice President of Consumer Education Maxine Sweet; Burson-Marsteller's Emily Hallford (Santa Monica) and Tracy Akselrud (Los Angeles); LowerMyBills.com; RMCN Credit Services' general manager Allen Humphris; Clinton Wade, Estate Agent, President's Circle, Prudential CA Realty, Pacific Design; Realtor Ron Roth, principal at Premier Realty; Linda Davis, RE/MAX Realty Group in Gales Ferry, CT; Realtor Kathi Frank RE/MAX, The Woodlands & Spring; RE/MAX Masters Broker-Associate in Texas, Nicole Smith; Zoey Farooq; Diane Saatchi, senior vice-president of The Corcoran Group in New York; Sherri Strickland, ABR (Accredited Buyer Representation), Real Estate Agent for Cornerstone Properties in Victoria, Texas; Craig Harrison, Twin Tower Realty in Richmond, Virginia; Ben

McCormick (thank you for sharing your story!); David Boone, first vice president of The Provident Bank; Norm Bour, host of the Real Estate and Finance Radio Show and a 25-year veteran of the world of finance; TransUnion, LLC's Steven R. Katz; Faye Brock, ABR, CRS, GRI, RRS, and Broker/owner of Century 21 Brock & Associates in Wilmington, NC; real estate agents Leslie and Bob Nichols of RE/MAX Professional Group in Houston, Texas; Lana Jo Matthis; Co-owner/broker associate for ReMax Cherry Creek, Inc., in Denver, Colorado, Jim Thoeming; Larry Melichar, president & CEO, CBS Home Real Estate in Nebraska; Reggie Marston; Home Inspections; Sheng Li; real estate agent Roberta Alford, Coldwell Banker Gundaker, St. Louis, Missouri; real estate agent Larry Wallenstein of RE/MAX Consultants Realty in Fort Lauderdale, Florida; Alex Elezai, Countrywide, Private Mortgage Banker; Tara Nicholle Nelson, Esq. and author of *The Savvy Woman's Homebuying Handbook*; Melanie Rembrandt, owner of Rembrandt Communications, LLC, in Howell, MI; Jeffrey P. Zane, Esquire, president of the Attorneys' Real Estate Council of Palm Beach County, Inc., Florida; Edelman's Daniel Webber and media strategist/supervisor John B. Moore; David Goldstein of AMBIC Building Inspection Consultants; Greg Bell, owner of Bell Inspection Service; ERA Realtor Teddy Goodson, ABR, CRS; Dan Osborn of Upstate Home Inspection Service in Upstate New York; John Brennan, President of Brennan Environmental, Inc.; Kate Walsh of Brennan Environmental, Inc.; Sandy Botkin CPA, Esq., a former IRS attorney, trainer of IRS attorneys and author of *Real Estate Tax Secrets of the Rich* (McGraw-Hill) and *Lower Your Taxes: BIG TIME* (McGraw-Hill); McGraw-Hill Publicity's Eric Trenkamp; Ronald Magas, president of Magas Media Consultants in Connecticut; Jack Farrar, public relations manager of Company Operated Regions RE/MAX International (CO); U.S. Legal Forms, Inc.'s Christine U. Kimes; Texas Real Estate Commission's Loretta DeHay; Joy Alafia, Standard Forms Manager, Real Estate Business Services, Inc., a subsidiary of the California Association of Realtor; Edra C. Anderson, Associate Counsel of the

Texas Association of Realtors; Jonathan Shapiro of American Home Lenders, Inc.; Lee Watts of Belkind Schrager & Assoc.; Linda O'Donnell, RE/MAX Signature in Chicago, IL; Stacey Lawson of the Texas Association of Realtors; Laura Denise Milkowski, VP, The LDM Team at Corcoran in New York; RE/MAX Real Estate Services Broker Stephen O'Hara; Christine M. Todd, chief executive officer for the Northern Virginia Association of Realtors; Salvatore I. Prividera Jr., director of communications & special projects at the New York State Association of Realtors; Kevin Brafford, director of communications at the North Carolina Association of Realtors; Candi Szela of the Oregon Association of Realtors; Jim Nathan of James David Nathan & Co. in Chicago, IL; Tammy Brookhouser of the Nebraska Realtors Association; John W Baker, ABR, CRS, GRI, SRES, e-Pro Ned Baker Real Estate Inc.; Tom Kilkenny, RM International, and Ellen Bitton, president and CEO, Park Avenue Mortgage Group, Inc.

Contents

Jntroduction

Welcome to *Buying Your House on a Shoestring*! This book shares so many great money-saving tips to help you through the home-buying process. It takes you step by step through how to get financing, improve your credit, find a home, negotiate the best deal, square away an inspection, compare your mortgage options, and have a hassle-free closing. We all go to work everyday, but when we get a chance to see our work turn into dream objects, such as a beautiful home we have dreamed of or a car we always wanted, all that work and all our accomplishments seem worth it. It's rewarding. Like anything, if you have good guidance, you will be able to make better decisions and have a better experience (that's why you should pick up this book). Just because you are buying one of the largest investments you may make in a lifetime does not mean it has to burn a hole in your pocket.

Did you know that today, many first-time homeowners don't have 20 percent to put down and many don't have perfect credit?

One afternoon, my friend Ben Arnold asked me, "What do you want folks to learn most from your book?"

We were in the middle of work and had stopped to chat.

I thought a moment. I was in the early stages of writing this book, and I replied, "That's a really good question, Ben."

"You know, I really want folks to know that their credit is the most important part to starting the home-owning process. The better your credit, the better interest you will get on a loan. Better loan options are available to you and, in the end, you will pay less on the life of that loan."

Honestly, credit is everything. (See Chapter 3. We talk with experts from Fair Isaac, the brains behind the credit-scoring system for advice. And, readers of *Buying Your House on a Shoestring* get a free credit help session with RMCN Credit Services.) If you have less than perfect credit, it's not the end of the world. A good friend of mine had gone through a lot after his wife passed away and his credit had fallen to the wayside; his eyes still tear up when he talks of her. When he decided to buy a home, his mortgage person helped him improve his credit situation. (You would be amazed how much mortgage lenders can help you; visit Chapter 2 to see how.) He was able to buy a home he is now so thankful for.

Before you get started, get pre-qualified or pre-approved for a loan. I highly recommend getting pre-approved for a loan. It's so important. You will find out exactly how much you can afford and you will be more financially set than the next guy who only has a pre-qualification letter that only estimates what he can afford. If you don't know where to turn to get pre-qualified or pre-approved, we partnered with Wells Fargo and Quicken Loans to help you! See Chapter 2. Quicken Loans also has a great Website and toll-free number just for our readers of *Buying Your House on a Shoestring* (see Chapter 2.)

We really want to help you with the home-buying process, to help make it is as easy and accessible as it can be.

We have so many great tips from scores of amazing Realtors, credit experts, mortgage pros, and inspectors. (Find out what inspections you have available to you and how to get the seller to pay for repairs, in Chapter 9.) These negotiating tips protect your interests and save you money. There is also a checklist to a hassle-free closing, like the best time to have a closing, so you skip a month's payment (see Chapter 7 and Chapter 10), and so much more—even small things you can do to your new home that will save you so much money (Chapter 16).

We are all on a budget; the goal is to help you find and buy the home of your dreams without breaking the bank. Enjoy *Buying a Home on a Shoestring*!

If you have any questions while going through the home-buying process, feel free to send me your questions at pipernichole@gmail.com.

All the best,
Piper

Chapter 1

Step-by-Step Home-Buying Guide: How Much House Can You Buy?

"Between us," David sighs heavily from a long day at work.

I nod, leaning in closer.

It took several months for David to find the house of his dreams. It was a two-story, more-than-he-wanted-to-pay personal castle. He worked out a few credit stumbles and he signed countless paperwork for his $200,000 mortgage. He joked that they may as well have drawn blood from his very arms.

"It was the day of closing and I found out I needed to pay $400 in closing costs. I wasn't expecting to pay anything," he sighs. He didn't know how he was going to come up with $400 at the last minute—he was tapped dry and it was a week away from payday. His closing had been pushed back three times and he wanted to close on this house so much. His lease was up on his apartment, his boxes were packed, and his wife and two kids were anxious to move.

He asked his supervisor for an advance on his paycheck. But his supervisor couldn't find the general manager of the company to approve it. So, his supervisor pulls\ed out her checkbook and wrote him a check for $400 to help him have his closing. So thankful and relieved, he promised to pay her back.

"I may reach in my pockets," he shows me his empty pockets. But, he says, "I am surrounded by angels."

Now, he's moving in. And, he can't wait to just collapse with relief on his bed. He says, "We're tired, but it's a good tired."

It is one of the most rewarding feelings to purchase something you love, especially a home; it almost makes all that working seem worthwhile. We want to help you find the house of your dreams—and save money doing it. *Buying a House on a Shoestring* will take you step by step through the home-buying process: how to improve your credit, get the best interest rate, score a mortgage, avoid financial no-no's, use smart house-hunting tactics, negotiate an offer, follow steps to a hassle-free closing, and so much more. Thanks so much for joining us. If you have any questions in your home-buying process, feel free to e-mail me at *pipernichole@gmail.com*.

10 Steps to Your New Home

We have an easy-to-understand overview of the home-buying process.

Step 1: How Much Can You Afford?

When making a large purchase there are a few main points you want to know to make the whole process easier: How much can you afford to purchase? And how much will you pay every month? How much cash will you need up front and are you prepared to buy? The easiest and most efficient way to find out how much house you can buy is to meet with a lender. Get pre-qualified (good) or pre-approved (better) for a loan. Lenders look at your credit history, income (before taxes), debts, assets, savings, and how much money you will have for your down payment, anywhere from five to 20 percent of the home's price. (There are also 0 to low down-payment options depending on your situation.)

⇨ **Pre-qualification**: You casually tell your lender how much money you make, your debts, credit history, and assets. In turn, they give you an estimate of how much you can afford. This option is non-binding to your lender—the financial information you shared isn't verified. Prequalification is typically free.

⇨ **Pre-approval**: If you are a serious buyer (and to be a competitive buyer) go with the pre-approval. This one is better. The lender verifies your credit history, employment, debts, and assets. You receive a letter that says your mortgage is approved for an exact amount (and is good for a certain time frame). Some lenders charge for a pre-approval.

Hot Tip:

"The best tip for buyers is not to be pre-qualified for a mortgage! Instead, get pre-approved! This puts the buyer in the best negotiating position. The strength of the buyer is important to the seller, and could make the difference in a multiple-offer situation. The process can take just a few days or, in some cases, a few hours. But once a buyer is pre-approved the seller knows the buyer is a qualified purchaser."

—Linda Davis, RE/MAX Realty Group in Gales Ferry, Connecticut

SHOESTRING TIP:

"When a person is considering buying a home it is very important they get pre-approved with a lender. Many sellers will not consider an offer without a pre-approval letter from a lender. Pre-approval is different from pre-qualified. Pre-approval means the lender has verified things like savings, FICO score, and employment. There are many programs available to first-time buyer's that make it easier for them to get into a home. Some of the most common are 100 percent financing, 5 percent down, and 10 percent down. By choosing one of these, it allows the buyer to get into a home with less savings. Also, it allows them to save more of their money for closing cost and unforeseen expenses. It is always good for buyers to have extra money at the close."

—Clinton Wade, Estate Agent, President's Circle, Prudential California Realty, PacificDesign Center, West Hollywood, California

⇨ **How much can you buy?** A general rule of thumb is you can afford a home that is about two-and-one-half times your yearly income. The best way to gauge how much you can buy is to talk with a lender, or, if you want a general idea, try one of the numerous calculators online (*Quicken.com*, *Ginniemae.gov*, *WellsFargo.com*, or *Realtor.com*, among many others) that can estimate what you can afford.

Your Debt-to-Income	**Housing Expense**
Your debt-to-income ratio should not be more than 36 percent of your gross income. Debt-to-income (back-end ratio) is how much of your gross income would go toward all your debts (mortgage, car loans, credit cards, student loans, child support, and alimony, among other debts). To see your debt-to-income: Multiply your annual salary by .36, divide by 12 (months) = max. debt to income ratio. Your total debt based on a $40,000 income would be $1,200 per month. Source: *Bankrate.com*	Do you want to know how much of your monthly income will go toward your monthly mortgage? Your mortgage payment should not be more than 28 percent of your pre-tax monthly income. To see how much you would pay in housing expenses per month: Multiply your yearly salary by .28 and divide by 12 (months) = maximum housing expense. If you made $40,000 a year x .28 divided by 12 = $933 max. housing expense.

⇨ **Other expenses considered**: The other expenses lenders look at when determining how much house you can buy are:

- Real estate taxes.
- Homeowner's insurance.
- Find out if there are special requirements for hazard insurance (for example, mandatory coverage for earthquakes, flood, and so on).
- If you put down less than 20 percent, many times you will have to get private mortgage insurance (PMI).

MONEY SAVER:

10 Don'ts When Applying for a Real Estate Loan

Realtor Kathi Frank gives her clients these 10 no-no's when applying for a real estate loan. These are the mistakes many buyer's make and what you can avoid.

1. Don't change jobs, become self-employed, or quit your job.
2. Don't buy a car, truck, or van (or you may be living in it!).
3. Don't use charge cards excessively or let your accounts fall behind.
4. Don't spend money you have set aside for closing.
5. Don't omit debts or liabilities from your loan application.
6. Don't buy furniture.
7. Don't originate any inquiries into your credit.
8. Don't make large deposits without first checking with your loan officer.
9. Don't charge bank accounts.
10. Don't co-sign a loan for anyone.

Hot Tip:

If your financial situation changes, let your lender know because this may affect how much you can afford to buy. To get pre-approved or pre-qualified, see Chapter 2.

Step 2: Deciding to Buy: Renting vs. Owning

"The primary reason for my buying a home was because renting in Boston has gotten very expensive, and I thought that instead of paying more than $2,000 in rent a month, I can use the money towards a mortgage."—Zoey Farooq

Zoey felt investing in property in the Boston area (with growing property values) was a good decision and she started looking for an apartment she felt did not need any repairs or maintenance. She says, "I have always lived in a professionally managed building and was looking for a place that will give me the same amenities but not break the bank." Then, while walking her dog half a block away from where she was living, she found what she was looking for. It was a remodeled older building and everything in the apartments was brand new. She knew she wouldn't have to worry about items breaking or not working.

If you are debating whether to rent or own, we talked with Diane Saatchi, who has experience in selling and renting homes for 15-plus years. This senior vice-president of The Corcoran Group in New York shares with us the pros and cons of renting versus buying on page 25.

Step 3: Let's Talk About Credit

My friend always says, "When you buy a home, your credit is more important than how much money you have saved up for a down payment." He is right. There are so many options lenders can help you with when it comes to down-payment help. But, a good credit score is priceless! It means a better interest rate, so you will pay less over the life of the loan. A credit score in the mid-700s will typically qualify you for the best loans and interest rates, says Craig Watts of Fair Isaac Corporation, the company behind the credit scoring system. Get a free copy of your credit report (one from each of the credit agencies yearly) from Experian, Equifax, and TransUnion at

The Pros and Cons of Renting vs. Buying

—Diane Saatchi

PROS TO BUYING

Long term, it is best to buy a home if you plan to live in it for many years. The benefits of owning a home are: appreciation: Value grows over time and your initial investment becomes more valuable. National Association of Realtor's former president Tom Stevens says, "Homeowners have a net worth almost 36 times more than that of renters," according to the Federal Reserve Board.Tax perk: Interest paid on a mortgage is tax deductible as are deductions for property taxes on federal tax returns, which reduces the cost of homeownership. Mortgage costs can be fixed while value and income increase.

CONS TO BUYING

Buying costs money: For example, closing costs can be as high as 10 percent of the purchase price. Also, it costs to sell. Short stay? With buying and selling costs, a short stay can be very expensive. Value can decrease over time: It is possible that one can loose money on a sale if it sells for less than purchase price. Repairs and maintenance: Can be expensive."Benefits to renting are the exact opposite of the cons to owning," says Diane. "It is especially wise to rent in any market if one is not certain of staying put for several years."

MONEY SAVER:

"During the past 10 years, the cost of rental housing in the United States has increased an average of 3 percent per year. That means an apartment or home that rents for $750 a month will cost more than $978 a month 10 years from now."

—Tom Stevens, former president of the National Association of Realtors. See the special interview with Tom Stevens in Chapter 15.

www.*annualcreditreport.com*. these credit reports don't come with the score. *MYFICO.com* charges for your three credit reports and scores, as well as how to improve it. You will want to check your credit report several months ahead of purchasing to know if there is anything you need to correct or improve.

Your credit report score is based on five main areas: payment history (35 percent), amounts you owe (30 percent), length of your credit history (15 percent), types of credit used (10 percent), and new credit (10 percent). The best advice: Make all your payments on time and pay down your balances (the lower your balance is compared to your limit, the better). Check for mistakes on your report, contact the credit bureau, and get it corrected.

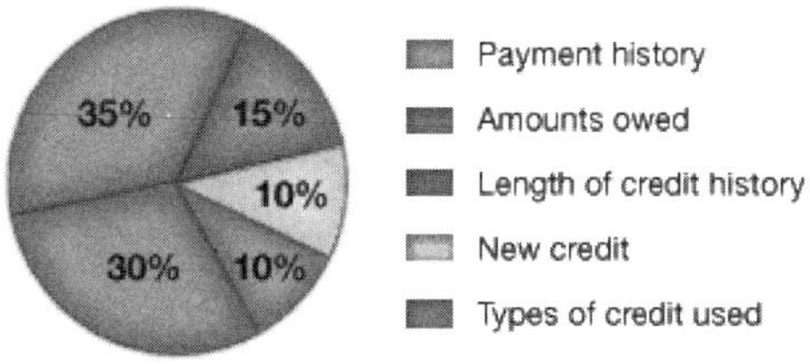

Insiders Insight

When folks come to you interested in buying a home, how do you get them rolling in the process?

"I always have buyers talk to a lender before paying off debts when they are contemplating buying a home. Sometimes, buyers choose the wrong debt to pay. A lender can be more instrumental in counseling the buyer to pay off the debts that will allow the buyer to get a lower interest rate or pay less money down.

"Lenders know which debts, when paid off, can raise credit scores more than others. A buyer may pay something off and have it do very little to raise the overall score. When this is the case, the money was basically wasted."

"When the buyer gets pre-qualified, then I pull a list of homes that meet the criteria the buyer's needs/wants and we get started with the selection process."

—Sherri Strickland, ABR
(Accredited Buyer Representation)
Real Estate Agent for Cornerstone Properties in Victoria, Texas

Maxine Sweet, vice president of consumer education at Experian, says, "Lenders price their services according to risk. The higher your risk, the more likely you won't pay as agreed." If you have good credit, she says, "You will pay lower interest and perhaps be offered more attractive terms, such as a higher limit, lower down payment." A low credit score can also cost you when it comes to home insurance. Visit Chapter 3 for a *free* personal credit help session and tips on how to improve your credit.

Step 4: Home-buying Costs to Expect

There is nothing more terrifying to home buyers than:

1. The cost of a house.
2. Applying for a loan to pay for it.
3. Paying out of pocket at closing.

So, to ease your mind up front about costs associated with home buying, we're going to go over key costs to expect.

"A first-time buyer typically pays for things such as the home inspection and appraisal during the escrow. This runs several hundred dollars," says Clinton Wade. "At the closing,

SHOESTRING TIP:

What if you need help with closing costs?"If a buyer does not have enough money for closing cost they can ask for a credit from the seller to go towards non-recurring closing cost. This should be included in the original offer to the seller. It is best to be up-front about the situation because the seller typically asks for verification of funds to close. If the seller understands the situation and the lender feels they can get the loan, most are comfortable with this. Submitting this type of offer typically works best in a buyer's market when there is a surplus of inventory. In a seller's market the inventory is low and multiple offers are common. In a multiple offer situation, 100 percent financing and credits towards closing cost are not seen as strong offers. The more money a buyer is able to put down the stronger the offer is—it helps with things like appraisal and the ease of obtaining a loan."

—Clinton Wade, Estate Agent,
President's Circle,
Prudential California Realty,
Pacific Design Center, West Hollywood, CA

the buyer needs to have enough money for closing costs. Closing costs are made up of things such as deposit, escrow fees, title, and taxes. The seller typically pays the broker's commission."

⇨ **Closing costs**: Closing costs may include attorney fees, loan fees, appraisal costs, inspection fees, and the cost of a title search. For a complete list of closing costs, visit Chapter 2.

⇨ **Down payment**: While lenders like to see 20 percent as a down payment, many cannot afford that. Some private and public organizations, such as FHA (Federal Housing Administration), Freddie Mac, Fannie Mae, and the Department of Veteran Affairs, offer low down-payment mortgages. It is possible to pay three percent or less up front for a loan, if you qualify. However, if your down payment is less than 20 percent, you will have to pay for private mortgage insurance (PMI). But, another option lenders are giving buyers is "piggyback loans" (second loans that tend to be home equity loans or lines of credit for 10 to 15 percent of the home's price, according to CNN Money) that cover part of the down payment and avoid PMI.

MONEY SAVER:

"Home buyers have access to so many different mortgage products today, many of which no longer require a 20-percent down payment," says Tom Stevens of the National Association of Realtors president. "While standard, fixed-rate mortgages still exist, many people 'piggyback' these loans with other mortgages, reducing the amount of down payment required—in some cases, 100-percent financing can be arranged."

⇨ **Strapped for cash?** What if your cash on hand doesn't cover your needs? CNN Money recommends the four following options: 1.) If you're a first-time homebuyer and if you have an Individual

Retirement Account, you can withdraw up to $10,000. But, you have to pay taxes on what you withdraw. 2.) You can get a cash gift up to $12,000 a year from each of your parents (and your spouse's parents)—and it doesn't trigger a gift tax. 3.) Can your employer help? Some large employers can help you get a low-interest loan (from select lenders) or help with the down payment. 4.) You can use your 401(k) or retirement plan that's similar to taking a loan out from yourself or make a withdrawal.

⇨ **Unexpected expenses to consider:** Clinton says, "Some unexpected homeowner expenses to consider are things like yard maintenance, homeowner dues (condo), repairs (roof/plumbing/electrical), and assessments (if you are purchasing a condo). With a condo it is always good to find out how much money the home owners association has in reserves. This will help you understand the likelihood of an assessment. The less they have in reserves the more likely an assessment is."

Word Alert

Down payment: When you buy an expensive large item such as a home or car, you typically make a down payment up front with the purchase. In some cases, there are programs and options to help you avoid paying down payment out of your pocket. Talk with your mortgage person to help you.

Closing costs: Closing costs (or "settlement costs") are fees associated with purchasing a property. For example, closing costs are usually made up of a loan origination fee, appraisal fee, credit report charges, title search, title insurance, discount points, taxes, and deed-recording fee, among other fees.

Step 5: Selecting Your Entourage

You will need a Realtor, lender, home inspector, and closing agent (attorney or title/settlement company) looking out for your needs. First, start with finding your Realtor. A lot of times, buyers find the house of their dreams and ask the seller's Realtor,

Sample Closing Costs

Transfer Taxes	Varies widely by state and municipality
Loan Discount Points	Generally 0–2 percent of loan
Title Company Closing Fee	$150–$400
Buyer's Attorney Fee	$400 and up
Lender's Attorney Fee	$150–$500
Title Insurance (Lender's Policy)	Varies: generally between $175–$875
Homeowner's Insurance	Varies: $300 and up
Underwriting Fee	$195–$795
Survey Fee	$150–$400
Home Inspection	$225–$450
Pest Inspection	$75
Down Payment	Varies widely
Flood Determination/Life of Loan Coverage	$19.50
Recording Fees	Varies widely depending on municipality. Generally between $50 and $150.
Courier Fee	$30
Prepaid Interest	Varies depending on loan amount, interest rate, and time of month you close on your loan.

Source: Quicken Loans

representing the home, to be their agent, too. You really want a Realtor representing you—a buyer's agent—who is looking out for your best interests in the transaction. Clinton says to make sure to check the Realtor's references. Clinton says, "Getting a referral from a friend or family member who has gone through the process is a good way to choose an agent. It is a good idea to interview several agents and go with the one with whom you are most comfortable. Be sure you check references!" Just ask Faye Brock. More than half her business comes from referrals. If you don't have recommendations to fall back on, look at the area in which you're interested and notice which Realtors have the most signs posted in the area—that is a good indication they are familiar with the area. Interview Realtors before selecting one to represent you. For more on how to find a great Realtor, visit Chapter 4.

Here are some quick links to check out to get you warmed up in the search process; by all means, don't stop here. If you've tapped out referrals or want to start your search online, check out these top-notch sites.

Searching for a Realtor: You can search for a Realtor at *www.Realtor.com*, run by the National Association of Realtors. You can also find and compare Realtors at *HomeGain.com* or Yahoo! Real Estate, and there are many other options.

Need a lender: Shop. Shop. Shop. Look for the best interest rates and the best products suited to your needs. For an extensive list of lenders in your area, visit Fannie Mae's "Find a Lender" search at: *www.mortgagecontent.net/flApplication/fanniemae/findLender.jsp*. To see the difference between working with a banker, mortgage broker, or lender, visit Chapter 2.

Home inspector wanted: Some recommend against your Realtor recommending an inspector. But, sometimes, Realtors know who is the best to contact because they've had experience working with them. Find a listing of inspectors in your area (interview them and see a copy of their inspection report). Each of the national associations for home inspectors have search options to find a home inspector in your zip code. Visit: *www.ashi.org*, *www.nachi.org*, and *www.nahi.org*.

Real estate attorney: When selecting an attorney to handle your closing or help with the contract, look into having an attorney who specializes in real estate. Visit *www.findlaw.com*. Title and escrow companies also serve as an alternative to a real estate attorney in handling closings.

Step 6: Finding Your Dream House

Realtor Diane Saatchi, senior vice president of The Corcoran Group in New York, says there are three no-no's when home buying:

1. Don't fall in love with a house: Fall in love with a location.
2. Don't shop for a home until you are certain of a budget. Know how much cash is available for a down payment, how much a lender will extend for a mortgage, and how much you can pay per month (now and over the next several years).
3. Don't be fooled by good décor; don't be turned off by bad décor.

When you are looking at potential homes always get a comparable market analysis from your Realtor. It will tell you the details of the house: how many bedrooms, bathrooms, kitchen, and so on., square footage, how much it sold for before, how long it has been on the market, and so much more. It gives you the intimate details of the home, and you find out what other homes nearby have sold for recently to see if the asking price is overpriced, underpriced, or just right. While you browse newspaper ads, open houses, Realtor recommendations, you can also search online—the biggest listing of homes available for sale online is at the National Association of Realtors Website at *www.Realtor.com*. Another interesting site that shows you a home's estimated market value price is *www.zillow.com*

(worth a click through). Make sure you let your Realtor know exactly what you are looking for in a home, so they find the house that is right for you.

"The most difficult aspect to buying a home is finding one that suits your needs," says Clinton. "A buyer must realize that they are not going to get everything they want, they must be willing to make sacrifices. The most important decision a buyer can make when purchasing a home is making sure they are represented by someone who understands the process from beginning to end."

Step 7: Making an Offer

You've found your dream home and you want to make an offer on it, Realtor Ron Roth, principal at Premier Realty, gives us these tips for negotiating:

- First, know that the first step in putting yourself in the proper negotiating position is to hire an agent to best represent your interests.
- Know what is important to you and what is important to the seller.
- Be prepared when writing your offer! Have all of your financing figured out and be pre-approved. You can be the highest priced offer, but if the seller has no idea how you are getting the money, you will instantly be put in a weaker position.
- Know what the market is bearing:

  Seller's market (more buyers than sellers): You probably won't get the property for much less than asking (if not more than asking). Your competition will come from other buyers, so negotiate accordingly. You may have to raise your level of competitiveness in order to make yourself the most attractive buyer in the eyes of the seller.

  Buyer's market: Your competition is the seller. Find out what is important to the seller, price or terms. If price is more important to you, and terms are more important to the seller, then offer attractive terms and be firm on price. If vice versa, then do the opposite. Terms for the seller may be that he/she may have to sell very quickly or just the opposite. He/she may be building a house and may need to stay on the property for an extra three or four months. The seller may be wary of 100-percent financing and, therefore, may be willing to accept a lower price with more money down.

The offer "presentation" has an effect as well. Does it include a pre-approval letter, your credit scores, proof of funds, a copy of the deposit check, a letter from the buyer to the seller? How does the offer look aesthetically? Is it poorly written, or is it neatly typed? Is it computer generated?

All of these things have a profound impression on the seller and their agent. They would much rather work with a buyer (and their agent) if the offer is neat and professional because it may be a good indication of how the sale will proceed. A sloppy offer and presentation is a good indication that things may go drastically wrong when trying to close.

Step 8: What the Home Inspection Reveals

After an offer has been accepted, many times, the contract will be contingent on a whole house inspection. This is one of the most important aspects of the transaction, because you will get a chance to find out what is wrong with the house and request the seller to make repairs. Linda Davis, Realtor for RE/MAX in Connecticut, says, "My 30 years of experience has been that sellers are generally reasonable if the requests are legitimate and documented." (See Chapter 9.)

Step 9: Before Closing

After the paperwork has been signed, the most important aspects to take care of before closing are: finalize financing, set up the inspection (and any additional inspections), get homeowner's insurance, make sure you have someone handling your closing, make sure the seller has the termite inspection done (and takes care of any problems), and attend the final walk-through.

The home appraisal will also be done, along with a title search (usually handled by your lender).

Before you close on the house, your mortgage person will give you what's called a "good faith estimate." It lists the closing costs (usually between two and 10 percent of your loan). The letter will give you a settlement statement (or closing statement), showing you all of the final costs in the transaction. You can see this statement a day before closing to avoid surprises or mistakes.

The final step is the closing or settlement. For a complete 'to-do' list before closing, visit Chapter 10.

Step 10: Closing!

If I were to describe closing to you simply, and from the eyes of a buyer, you walk into the office of the person who is handling your closing (be it your attorney, title company, or escrow company). There is a huge stack of papers on the desk. Among the primary documents you will sign during the closing:

- ✓ Settlement statement.
- ✓ Contract.
- ✓ Loan documents.
- ✓ Title or deed.
- ✓ Homeowner's insurance.
- ✓ Payoffs of your existing mortgage (if applicable).
- ✓ Down payment and closing costs.

Most buyers nod silently as the closing agent walks them through the paperwork, signing their John Hancock, knowing that once they reach the bottom of the stack of papers, the keys will finally be in their hands.

Closing is where the title of the house is transferred to your name and you finally get the keys to your new home. Closing varies from state to state. In some places sellers, buyers, and their Realtors will attend the closing. In other areas, only the buyers are present. The closing usually takes place in an attorney's office, title company, or an escrow company.

Starting Your Home-Buying Adventure

Deciding if you want to buy a home is a personal decision. There are other factors involved: your lifestyle, saving your child's college fund, retirement, leisure, and entertainment (traveling, going out to dinner, etc.) that are also important. Will you be able to afford this and your house payment comfortably? Do you want to handle (and do you have a nest egg for) repairs and maintenance every time there is a leaky sink, broken pipe, running toilet, broken refrigerator? There won't be a landlord to turn to. Are you ready to take on those extra chores?

On the flip side, there are many perks to home ownership. "One of the most obvious advantages to home ownership is you can deduct property taxes and mortgage interest from your annual taxes—think of it as a forced saving account. Secondly, you are not throwing away money on rent—you are investing in your future," says Clinton. "Home ownership is an exciting adventure if you understand what you are embarking on."

Your Budget Worksheet

How much you can afford is based on your income (before taxes), savings, debt, and monthly payments. We have a few worksheets and tips from Ginnie Mae below to help calculate your expenses. Determine how much you spend each month on bills, how much you need for you (family vacation, mini-trips, movie outings, restaurants, and the little things that keep you happy from day to day), and how much you feel comfortable paying each month for a house. Twin Tower Realty Realtor Craig Harrison always tells his clients that they don't have to buy the max they can afford. He says, "You never know when you may need a buffer for house repairs and other things that come up unexpectedly." On pages 37–39, you can calculate your monthly income, savings, monthly expenses and debt. Enter the four totals you get in the affordability calculator at *www.ginniemae.gov* to see an estimate of how much you can afford. Once you know how much you can afford and how much you are willing to pay monthly for a house (and for how long), you will enjoy the search for your new home!

Monthly Income

Review all your sources of income. You will need money for a down payment and closing costs. Federal House Administration and Vetran's Administration have mortgage programs that require smaller down payments. Closing costs may sometimes be rolled into the mortgage. Estimate your monthly income.

Income Category	Monthly
Borrower's Salary	$________
Co-Borrower's Salary	$________
Taxable Interest	$________
Investment Dividends	$________
Other Income	$________
TOTAL:	$________

Savings

Add up your savings. Any money saved can help you buy a home. Your savings can be used to pay the down payment and/or closing costs. You know your own saving habits.

Savings Category	Monthly
Savings Account	$ ______
Checking Account	$ ______
Retirement Fund Contributions	$ ______
Stock, Mutual Fund Investments	$ ______
Other Savings	$ ______
TOTAL:	$ ______

Monthly Expenses

You can expect your monthly expenses to go up when you buy a home. Will you have enough money to pay the mortgage, insurance, and property tax in addition to your other expenses?

Expense Category	Monthly
Utilities	$ ______
Car Expenses	$ ______
Insurance	$ ______
Medical Expenses	$ ______
Clothing	$ ______
Taxes	$ ______
Entertainment/Purchases	$ ______
Child Support	$ ______
TOTAL:	$ ______

Debt

A lender will examine your debt-to-income ratio to determine how much money to lend you.

Debt Category	Monthly
Credit Card	$ ______
Car Loans	$ ______
School Loans	$ ______
Alimony	$ ______
Child Support	$ ______
Other Personal Debt	$ ______
TOTAL:	$ ______

Now, enter these four totals into the affordability calculator at *www.ginniemae.gov* to see an estimate of how much you can afford. (The estimate is based on if you are married with two dependents.) (Source: *GinnieMae.gov*)

Chapter 2

Meeting With a Mortgage Officer: Getting Your Financial House in Order

How many times do we take a chance? A risk. A dare. That one moment that defines us and changes the course of our life. One day, Ben McCormick decided to pack up everything he owned in his Subaru—his beloved golf clubs, laptop, clothes, digital camera—and drove across the country from Baltimore, Maryland, to his dream destination of the Rocky Mountains of Colorado. Without knowing where he would live or what job he would find, he did it and succeeded; it was the one place he dreamed of moving to for years.

So, when he said, "I want to buy a house in Colorado," he meant it.

He checked his credit report months before deciding to buy. Because he does have great credit, and being a first-time home-buyer also helped, most of his approval for his loan was based on the strength of his credit. He had changed jobs recently, and usually lenders like to see longer job history. He knew he wanted a home at the time because interest rates were still good and it was still a buyer's market.

During three to four months of off-and-on again searching, Ben focused on location—the West Highlands area of Denver. He wanted a good location in the city, one that was close to the action with places he could walk to. It was also important to find a good home that didn't need a lot of work. And one day, he found that good home with two bedrooms, a garage, patio, and beautiful hardwood floors. It was in the city with a lot of new development and it meant a lot to him when he saw a mother walking down the street with a baby stroller; he knew it was a safe area.

Now, he is within walking distance of a barbershop, a place to get groceries, coffee shop, great restaurants, other shops, and an old hardware store, where he can now pick up paint for his new home.

He says that getting pre-approved for the loan was the easy part. It was the unexpected expenses while going through the home-buying process that he wants to warn others about. When you make an offer on a house and write a check for the earnest money deposit, it gets cashed soon after; the cost of the home inspection comes out of your pocket. Unexpected closing costs (he found out that he would have to pay a year's worth of taxes and homeowner's insurance upfront that would be held in escrow) made the difference between his closing costs $3,000 to $5,000. He admits, it was almost a deal breaker. But, it all worked out.

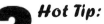

Hot Tip:

"Look at your entire budget, not just what you get approved for."

—Ben McCormick

SHOESTRING TIP:

"Get a good faith estimate of closing costs ahead of time from your lender and any miscellaneous expenses, like home inspection fees, from your Realtor."

—Teesie Howell, senior loan officer for National City Mortgage in Richmond, Virginia

He loves his new home and he says, "It's exciting when you have a little piece of the American dream."

First Steps if You're Thinking of Buying

Teesie Howell says to make sure your credit is in order. The senior loan officer for National City Mortgage in Richmond, Virginia, says if you've never had any credit or if you ever had credit

problems (such as coming-out-of-college debt or going through a divorce), check your credit report and make sure there are no surprises. Request your credit report online at *www.annualcreditreport.com.* If you find any errors on it, report the correction to all three credit bureaus: Equifax, Experian and TransUnion. Teesie says if you don't feel comfortable reporting the incorrect information to the credit bureau yourself, get a loan officer or another financial professional to walk you through it. Teesie shares the following straightforward financial pointers if you're thinking of buying:

-  Don't have your credit cards maxed out at their limits. Say you have a $2,500 limit; you don't want the balance to be $2,500. You want the balance to be well under the limit.
- Pay off past due accounts, collections, judgments, and tax liens.
- Be sure you have credit, "which tends to be a problem with young people and immigrants, who work hard, but often don't believe in borrowing," says Teesie. Establish credit, even if you open up a couple of charge cards and only put $10 on each and pay it off every month. Do it in advance of buying. So next year, you have established a year's worth of credit.
- If you don't have credit, sometimes lenders can help you. They work with you to build alternative credit references, such as rental payment history, cell-phone payments, renter's insurance, health-club membership, utilities, and so on.
- Most people aren't aware that if you make corrections to your credit report, it usually takes 60 days for your credit report to improve. Your credit score won't improve overnight.

Defer Major Purchases

Teesie says to defer major purchases such as new cars, boats or, items of that nature. If you get a car loan, it definitely counts against you. Get the BIG thing first—the house. Then, purchase the car or boat. "Do it after you close," says Teesie. For example, if you qualify for a certain amount to get your dream house, but you buy a car before closing, it changes the amount you can afford for a home and you may not be able to get a loan for the same amount to get your dream home. So, hold off on such purchases until after closing. After closing then you can update that car. (Financing for vehicles is different than financing for homes.)

"I am currently in a transaction with first time-buyer's. They are a young couple with a six-month-old baby. They cannot afford anything over $400,000. Because my market is Los Angeles (West Hollywood), that means they could afford a one-bedroom condo. They had to take into consideration things like square footage, location, payment, and monthly homeowner dues. They ended up deciding on a 798-square-foot condo with monthly dues of $269. They would have preferred a two-bedroom condo but this is all they could afford. They wanted to get into a home and decided they would sacrifice for a few years to own their own home. The husband's credit was not great; however, the wife's credit was good. They decided to only have the wife apply for the loan so they would get a better rate, thus giving them a lower monthly payment. They also decided to do 100 percent financing so they would have money left over for things like closing cost's, repairs, and their newborn baby. Together they have a combined income of $106,000 per year.

"Most first-time buyers must realize they cannot afford their dream home when first starting out. The most important thing they can do is get their foot in the door and build equity. Then, after a few years, they can move on to a larger property and keep doing that until they are able to afford their dream home. There is a certain amount of risk one must take when buying a home; however, it should be a calculated risk. If you don't take the plunge you will never reap the rewards."

—Clinton Wade, Estate Agent, President's Circle, Prudential California Realty, Pacific Design Center, West Hollywood, California

Getting Financially Set to Buy

Find a lender before house hunting. They will help you get pre-qualified or pre-approved for a mortgage loan. (Note: Getting pre-approved is always better.) You find out how much you can afford to buy. Then, when you make an offer on a home and give them your pre-approval or pre-qualification letter, the seller knows you are a serious buyer.

Pre-qualified means, as Teesie describes, "I've talked to you on the phone and pulled a credit report." You find out an estimate of what you can afford to buy.

Pre-approval is the way to go if you are a serious buyer. Say you went to Teesie to get pre-approved for a loan—meaning she verified your assets, income, pulled a credit report from all three credit-reporting agencies (not just one), and approved you for the loan, subject only to an appraisal. And, you know exactly how much you can borrow to buy a home.

"The best tip for buyers is not to be pre-qualified for a mortgage! Instead, get pre-approved! This puts the buyer in the best negotiating position. The strength of the buyer is important to the seller, and could make the difference in a multiple offer situation," says Linda Davis, RE/MAX Realty Group in eastern Connecticut. "The process can take just a few days or in some cases a few hours, but once a buyer is pre-approved, the seller knows the buyer is a qualified purchaser."

Start Gathering This Paperwork

When you are getting ready to meet with a lender to apply for a loan application, it usually requires the following items (you may want to start gathering this together early on):

Employment information:

- Current employer's name and address. If you have been working less than two years, they will require your previous employer's contact information.
- Two years of W2s.
- Recent pay stubs (1 month's worth).
- Self-employment: Federal tax returns (last two years), as well as current profit and loss statements. Also for commissions, interest/dividends, bonuses, rental income—if income is needed for you to qualify.
- Alimony/child support: If you want to disclose income from child support or alimony, provide a copy of the divorce decree or separation agreement or court order, plus proof of payment.
- Students: If you were in school for the past two years and you weren't working full time, you will need to provide your transcripts or diploma.

> **SHOESTRING PERK:**
>
> 
>
> **Helping You Get Financing for Your Home**
>
> If you would like to get pre-approved or pre-qualified, we partnered with Quicken Loans to help you. Quicken Loans is offering a special Website, *www.quickenloans.com/shoestring*, or call (800)-962-1644, just for readers of *Buying Your House on a Shoestring* who are seeking an asset-verified mortgage approval.

Assets:

- Recent statements for the past two months (checking, savings, money market, and CD accounts).
- Account statements for stocks, bonds, and mutual funds.
- Any real estate you own: current leases, lender information, and a copy of the deed, if you own it.

Liabilities:

- Your address for the past two years.
- Mortgage loan information.
- Credit cards and charges.
- Rental information.
- Child support and alimony payments.

Lenders can help you find a mortgage that suits your financial needs. If you find out your credit needs help or if you have questions about the process, a good loan officer is priceless. When you find out how much you can afford to buy, you can see what fits your budget comfortably and you don't waste your time looking at homes that cost more than you can afford. You may even find you can afford more than you thought. The key is finding a good loan officer who:

1. Understands your needs.
2. Understands your financial situation.
3. Is able to find a mortgage that works for you.
4. Will work with you and can be trusted.

SHOESTRING TIP:

If you are a first-time homeowner, you can contact your local state housing authority or visit *www.hud.gov/local/index.cfm* for a listing of first-time homeowner and down payment assistance programs for each state.

The Art of a Good Lender

The key is to look for a reliable, smart lender who has been in the business and who can help you find a loan that suits your needs. You can work with mortgage brokers, mortgage bankers, or banks. The best is asking for referrals from friends and family (or ask your Realtor for recommendations). While we wish Teesie was in every hometown, she does recommend what to look for in a lender:

- ✓ Do they return your calls?
- ✓ Do they walk you through a written good faith estimate?
- ✓ Are they offering you options?
- ✓ Are they willing to meet with you in person?
- ✓ Are they recommended by a reputable Realtor?
- ✓ How long have they been in the business?

"There are many different types of companies that offer home mortgage loans," says David Boone, first vice president of The Provident Bank. "There are the mortgage brokers, the mortgage bankers, and banks. There are pros and cons for deals with each type of company."

Mortgage Broker	
Pros	**Cons**
"They sometimes have access to many more lending products than the mortgage banker or banks. If a borrower is looking for an unusual mortgage product for an unusual property under unusual circumstances, the broker may be the best source for a mortgage. Extreme example: No money down, stated income, stated asset, low credit score, 4 family, pay-option ARM.	A mortgage broker has no ability to grant credit on their own. They are brokering the loan to someone else and making additional fees that the borrower pays for the loan. Therefore to work with a broker a borrower will pay the highest costs to obtain the mortgage. The loan will be serviced by someone else."
Mortgage Banker	
Pros	**Cons**
"They approve mortgages and close them in their own name. Because this is their only business, they tend to be experts at it. They also have the ability to broker loans if you need an unusual product," says Teesie.	"Lender has the option to sell the servicing of your loan to another lender after closing (but often doesn't)," says Teesie.
Banks	
Pros	**Cons**
"A bank usually has the mortgage products with the lowest fees," says David.	"A bank may not offer all types of loans or be able to finance all borrowers," says David. Teesie adds that "mortgages are not their only business, so at some companies you may not get the level of expertise or service you'd get with a mortgage banker."

Paying What You Can Afford

"They have to be comfortable in what they pay regardless of what they can qualify for. We see the two extremes. We have people who come in that don't understand why they can't qualify for x-sales price and x-payment when we tell them they qualify for less. Then, we have the opposite: we tell them they qualify for x and they say: 'I don't want that much of a payment.'"

—Teesie

When Twin Tower Realty Realtor Craig Harrison talks with his clients, he makes sure they speak with a mortgage lender first. His biggest rule of thumb is telling his clients to not buy as much as they qualify for, because there will be those unexpected house maintenance problems that pop up that you will have to pay for or the winter heating bill that you're not expecting when you purchase your home in the summer. Also, as Teesie wisely points out from her years in the mortgage industry, there are things that don't get included in qualifying: It doesn't include life insurance, education costs (if your kids go to private school or if they are in college), and so on. She says, "You need to take your personal lifestyle into account." (See Chapter 1 for a list of sample closing costs to expect.)

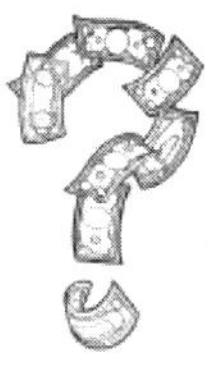

Q & A: Shoestring Budget Tips

You're on a shoestring budget and you want to know ways to save money when buying. We spoke with real estate broker Sherri Strickland of Cornerstone Properties in Victoria, Texas.

Piper: You're on a shoestring budget, what are ways you can save money when buying?

Sherri: You can use FHA or conventional financing that will allow you to finance in most of your closing costs. But, make sure you *do not* over extend yourself where your monthly payment is concerned. You know what *you* are comfortable with paying monthly. Lenders will traditionally lend you more than you are comfortable with where your payment is concerned. You don't want to have to stay home and "eat beans" because you cannot afford anything extra. There are costs that go along with home ownership that you do not have as a tenant, that is, all utilities, repairs, and general maintenance. A lender does not consider these additional costs when qualifying you for a home loan. You may ask the seller to pay closing costs for you. Ask your Realtor how long a property has been on the market. A newly listed seller will not be as motivated to help entice a buyer as one who has had his home on the market for an extended period of time.

Piper: What are financial no-no's when home buying?

Sherri: Again, do not overextend yourself. Do *not* take the first offer a lender makes; you do have some bargaining power with lenders. Shop around and make sure you let the lenders know you are shopping around. Make sure you get the lowest closing costs and the lowest interest rate available in your area. Some of the closing costs are considered "garbage fees." These are fees that lenders tack on to loans to make more money. Ask your chosen lender to remove these fees.

Piper: How much will buying a home cost you out of pocket?

Sherri: Traditionally 3 percent of the sales price if the seller can/will pay all of the allowable buyer's costs and you go with an FHA loan. There are many different types of loans out there for every buyer to have a different loan on any given day. Just make sure to take time out to educate yourself and shop around.

MONEY SAVER:

"There are 100 percent financing loans available for people with good credit!"

—Teesie Howell, Senior Loan Officer
National City Mortgage

Common Sense Things to Consider When Buying

> **SHOESTRING PERK:**
>
> **Do you want to know how much you can afford?**
>
> 
>
> You can fill out the easy form in the back of this chapter from Wells Fargo to get pre-approved or pre-qualified for a loan.

Teesie recommends a few pointers to keep in mind:

- How long do you plan on being in the house? For example, will you be in the house for a short time like two to three years because you know you're going to transfer? Maybe an adjustable rate mortgage (ARM) would be good. Or, do you plan to live in the home for many years? If you know your income will be the same for the next few years, maybe a 15- or 30-year fixed mortgage works better for you.
- Prepayment penalties: Most loans don't have pre-payment penalties unless you're doing a B or C mortgage (see what B or C mortgage means below in the Q&A). Many of these loans have prepayment penalties.
- Out-of-pocket costs: Even if you get 100 percent financing, you still have to pay closing costs and closing costs can be substantial. Sometimes, you can ask a seller to contribute toward closing costs, depending on the down payment and program; it varies how much a seller can contribute toward closing costs. But, Teesie says a good rule of thumb on a conventional loan is:

  - If the buyer gives 5 percent for a down payment, the seller can contribute up to 3 percent in closing costs.
  - If the buyer gives 10 percet on a down payment, the seller could contribute up to 6 percent in closing costs. Teesie says, "It's a rule of thumb, but it changes from product to product."

Hot Tip:

What kinds of mortgage customers are out there? How are their needs different? How can each be helped?

"Most mortgage customers have issues in two areas:

1. Down payment. As a society, we don't know how to save money.
2. Credit. Many kids were never taught that "if you borrow, you need to pay it back."

—David Boone, First Vice President of The Provident Bank

Q&A

Norm Bour, host of the *Real Estate and Finance Radio Show* and a 25-year veteran of the world of finance, gives us financial tips we can use.

Piper: How should you financially prepare before buying a home?

Norm: Getting pre-qualified is a mandatory step, including pulling a credit report from all three repositories—Equifax, Experian, and TransUnion, verifying income and job history, plus knowing exactly how much down payment is available. For first-time buyers it's important to consider closing costs, including loan fees and pre-paid expenses, which can be considerable. For those "buying up" from a prior home, they must account for those same items in their available funds.

Piper: How have you seen folks affected by credit when home-buying?

Norm: There are three factors when purchasing a home: income, LTV (loan to value, that is, the amount of the down payment versus how much they are borrowing), and credit. Most of these factors can be determined up front before ever starting the process, and many times buyers are surprised when they see their credit reports, because almost 35 percent have errors. Sometimes these errors are minor, sometimes they are serious and can kill the deal from the onset.

MONEY SAVER:

If you have so-so or bad credit, would you be better off waiting and improving your credit or going ahead and getting a sub-prime loan? "The decision on this resides with the borrower. It's really according to what a rental apartment costs versus the cost of the mortgage."

—David Boone, First Vice President of The Provident Bank

Piper: What negatively affects your credit and how can you improve it? How heavily does credit weigh in the loan process? How does it affect the type of loan/interest rate you can qualify for?

Norm: The most obvious dings that are incurred are late payments, and the more and the longer, the worse it is. One 30-day-late is minor, but when you have multiples of that or 90-day-plus delinquent payments it can be deadly. Collections (debts deemed not paid and sent to a third-party collector) and charge-offs (where the creditor decided they could not collect and "wrote it off") have an even more damaging affect. In the eyes of a potential "grantor of credit," if they see that you *knowingly* had debts and refused to pay, it's an ominous sign.

There are various classes of credit, from "A paper" to sub-prime, with many other letters in between. To get the *best* rate you want 20 percent or more down, "full doc," that is, full documentation rather than "stated income," and fully documented "assets" along with A+ credit. Depending upon the severity of the credit or other missing pieces, you can see as much as a five to six percent difference in interest rates and proportionate payments.

Piper: How do you know if a lender if offering you a B or C paper loan? How would you describe A, B, or C loans?

Norm: The lines are sometimes blurred between A, B, or C paper. When you see the "advertised" rates of most lenders, those represent the *best* the lender has to offer. Another factor to consider are the loans fees, too, because most quoted rates are based on paying some type of origination fee. If the rate "seems" lower than you think it should, it may be because of your credit score. As a general rule, anything more than 700 (mid score from all three bureaus) gives you the best rate. From 620 to 699 will usually get you a little higher of a rate, and below 619 puts you in a poor position. Of course you can still get financing, but it may be expensive, and many times they will be hybrid loans, fixed for two or three years, then adjusting. These are known as 2/28 or 3/27 loans, and in most cases they have pre-payment penalties that hit you if you try to sell or refinance before they convert to ARMs.

SHOESTRING TIP:

How would you describe prime vs. sub-prime loan? "Sub-prime can be described as a loan that is missing one or more elements that are required on a prime loan. What I mean by this is a sub-prime loan is not just a loan with credit score under 620. It could also mean a 'stated income' or 'no income' verification loan. These types of loans have 'missing documentation' or poor credit profile and therefore carry a high rate/fees."

—David Boone, First Vice President of
The Provident Bank

"There are low documentation products for people with good credit that are not considered sub-prime."

—Teesie Howell, Senior Loan Officer
National City Mortgage

Piper: Do you have good examples of how credit affected folks?

Norm: I am in the process of helping some clients who had a 30-day mortgage late 10 months ago, plus multiple late payments and collections. They have since paid off their collections, but the credit report still shows them. I recommended they visit *www.annualcreditreport.com,* which is the one site encompassing all three bureaus. Annually you may view a copy of your report for free and contest any errors that are evident. They will contact the reported creditor to verify if their information is accurate, and if it is not it must be removed. The process takes 30 to 60 days or so. In the event of mortgage lates, waiting until after 12 months can reap a huge benefit in a better interest rate, so sometimes patience can offer huge rewards.

Piper: What do you feel folks should know?

Norm: In the world of money, you have to look at it like a game; if you do not know the rules you will never win. Credit is a game, and you must know the penalties that can be incurred, and how to get "bonus points," too. And don't think the game is fair; it is not. Mortgages are also a type of game and you must know these rules, too. This game has more variables and is harder to learn and most lessons are learned the hard way, by individual errors made along the way. A 30-year loan is not always the best way and there are acceleration methods that can teach you how to create you own rules, which is one of our primary goals, teaching you how to "Think like a Bank."

Get Pre-Approved or Pre-Qualified

If you would like to get pre-approved or pre-qualified for a loan, you can fill out this form for Wells Fargo to send to a local mortgage consultant. Or visit *www.WellsFargo.com* online.

REQUEST FOR INFORMATION

FAX TO:

, Wells Fargo Home Mortgage Consultant

About Me:

Name:

Date of Birth:

Street Address:

City: State: Zip:

*Home Phone: Business Phone:

*E-mail Address:

About the Co-Borrower (if there will be one):

Name:

Date of Birth:

Street Address:

City: State: Zip:

*Home Phone: Business Phone:

*E-mail Address:

About My Homebuying Plan (if Purchasing):

I am interested in buying: ☐ A Primary Residence ☐ A Second Home ☐ An Investment Property

I plan to buy or begin building: ☐ Within Three Months ☐ In Three to Six Months ☐ In Six Months to a Year

If you've already been house hunting, what is the: a) Estimated Purchase Price: $

b) Estimated Down Payment: $

c) Estimated Loan Amount: $

Authorization to Obtain Credit Report/Consent for Credit Check and Phone Call/E-mail

I/we grant permission to Wells Fargo Home Mortgage to obtain my/our credit report. I/we understand that an approval is subject to normal credit investigation and that a consumer credit report may be requested from one or more consumer reporting agencies. I/we understand that this is a request for information only and is not an application for a loan. Additional information will be required of me/us at such time as I/we decide to apply. Credit is subject to approval.

* By providing the home phone numbers and e-mail addresses above, I/we hereby authorize Wells Fargo Home Mortgage to contact me/us at my/our home phone numbers or e-mail addresses.

Borrower's Name (printed): Borrower's Signature and date:

Social Security Number:

Co-Borrower's Name (printed): Co-Borrower's Signature and date:

Social Security Number:

Chapter 3

Credit! Please Help… Jmproving and Understanding Your Credit

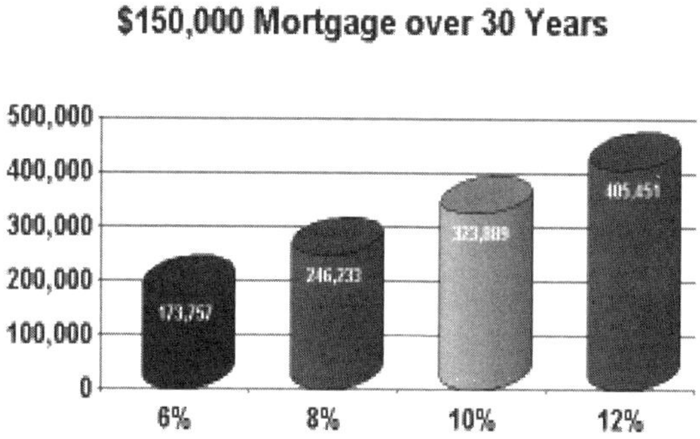

Allen Humphris has seen many people turn their troubled credit situation around to be able to buy a home. The general manager of RMCN Credit Services says it's just a matter of knowing what to do.

In this chapter, you'll find how to improve your credit score (the five crucial areas your score is based on), what your credit report says about you, fact vs. myths, repairing mistakes on your credit report, identity theft prevention, and how to get those free copies of your credit. Most importantly, you'll learn how to get credit to work for you.

> SHOESTRING PERK:
>
> **Free Credit Help Session**
>
> 
>
> Do you need help with your credit situation? Readers of *Buying Your House on a Shoestring* can have a free credit help session with RMCN Credit Services, Inc. Call: Allen Humphris, General Sales Manager at (972) 529-0900, ext. 251. E-mail: *a.humphris@rmcninc.com*.

How Do Credit Scores Work?

The idea behind credit scores is to determine your credit risk. Simple, huh? It's like loaning $20 to your friend who always pays you back versus your friend who never pays you back. Who would you loan money to and how much? Credit scores affect how much you can borrow and loan terms (such as interest rate). It can also play a role in how much you pay for insurance, whether you can replace your cell phone, and other financial decisions.

Your credit scores or FICO scores, which stands for Fair Isaac Corporation, the brains behind the scoring system, come from three main credit bureaus that each calculate your score: Equifax, Experian, and TransUnion. Each keep tabs on your financial

FICO Score Based on 5 Categories	Profile of Your Credit Report
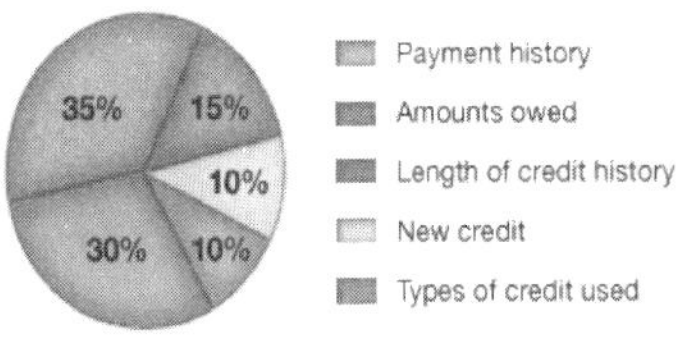	Identifying information: Name, address, social security number, date of birth, and employment to identify you.Trade lines: Your credit accounts. Date you opened the account, the account balance, and your payment history.Inquiries: List of everyone who pulled your credit report in the last two years. Public Record and collection items: Public record info from your state and county on overdue debt from collection agencies. Public record info includes: foreclosures, suits, wage attachments, liens, and judgments.

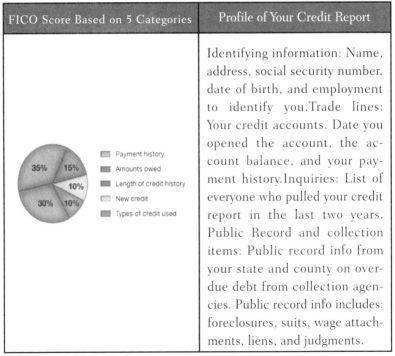

transactions. Mortgage lenders typically look at your score from each credit bureau and use your middle score. Others may purchase only one report and one score to make their decision.

Your FICO credit score is based on five main categories: Your payment history (35 percent), amounts you owe (30 percent), length of credit history (15 percent), types of credit used (10 percent), and new credit (10 percent). (These categories apply for all types of scoring models.)

Equifax will share your credit score with you. Experian and TransUnion will only allow *www.myfico.com* to convey FICO scores to you.

6 Steps to Better Credit

Before applying for a home mortgage loan, look at your credit report. You can get a free credit report each year from each of the credit bureaus (Equifax, Experian, and TransUnion) at *www.annualcreditreport.com*. Craig Watts of Fair Isaac Corporation says, "For most people, checking their credit reports and FICO scores six months before applying for a major loan will give them a good idea of their credit potential, and allow them sufficient time to correct genuine errors on the credit report and pay down any accounts with high balances before approaching lenders with loan applications." We have six steps to help you improve your credit.

Step 1: Pay Your Bills on Time

Your payment history: 35 percent of your credit score.

How much does a late payment cost you? It can lower your score by 50 to 100 points. Missing all your payments in a month can knock your score by more than 100 points. If you pay on time, it improves your score. When you're preparing to apply for a loan, it's especially important to pay all your bills on time. MyFICO says if you missed paying your bills, get current and stay current—and know that even if you pay off an account in collections, it will stay on your report for seven years.

Tip: "The most important message is that the only way to get a better score is to have a better credit history. That can't be changed overnight. The most important factor is to make all payments as agreed," says Maxine Sweet, vice president of public education at Experian. "If you have already missed payments, only time can make it better."

SHOESTRING PERK:

Do you have personal credit questions? You can ask Maxine Sweet, vice president of public education at Experian, by visiting *www.experian.com/ask_max.*

Step 2: Pay Down Your Credit Balances

Amounts you owe (your credit debt): 30 percent of your credit score.

Biggest mistake people make: "Running up high debt relative to their credit limit," says Watts of Fair Isaac. "And most people aren't aware that simply having high balances can really hurt their scores, because they assume lenders *like* high balances. Lenders might like it but risk scores don't."

Common mistake we make: Julie moves her debt around—transferring her credit card balance to another card. Then, she closes the paid-off card. Many do this. But, it's a big no-no, if it affects your credit balance to credit limit ratio.

For example, say you have three credit cards with a total credit limit of $6,000. You've charged $2,000. You've used one third of your credit limit. But, say you close out one card. Now, your credit limit totals $4,000—but, your credit debt is still $2,000. Now, it

Hot Tip:

"If your credit cards are at their limits, this can lower your credit score—even if the amount you owe isn't large."

—Freddie Mac

Visit *www.freddiemac.com*.

shows you've used half of your credit limit, making your score lower. If you are using a lot of your available credit, it may reflect that you are overextended and may have trouble paying your bills.

Tip: An important factor you can address right away is to pay down your balances. This reduces your credit utilization rate and your total outstanding debt, both of which are positives, says Sweet of Experian. "However, you shouldn't expect to see an overnight change. It often takes a few months, after your payment pattern has stabilized, to see an improvement in your risk score." When you pay down your balances, you can negotiate lower interest rates on your cards.

> **SHOESTRING TIP:**
>
> "I often find I need to explain to active credit-card users that paying their credit cards off entirely every month doesn't mean that their credit reports will show zero or even low balances for those accounts. That's because lenders typically report to the credit bureaus the most recent outstanding balance that was billed to the consumer. And active card users often show a sizeable balance-owed on their credit card bills. So it may not be enough to pay down the balance, the person also may want to use that card very sparingly (or not at all) for the last couple of months prior to applying for the loan, for purposes of improving their FICO score."
>
> —Craig Watts, Fair Isaac

Bottom line: Experts say pay off your debt, don't move it around.

Credit Scenario #1: Ariel pays her credit cards on time, but has high balances on five out of seven cards (near $3,000 in credit-card debt). She has about $2,900 remaining on her car loan and a $3,000 college loan. Two past college accounts are in collections (total: $950) but, she's on a payment plan. Plus, $2,100 in back state taxes she is on a payment plan with. How long will it take her to improve her credit and what should she do?

RMCN'S Advice: The best way to increase her credit score is to pay off revolving accounts in their entirety. If this is not an option, she should try to consolidate all revolving accounts. Depending on how fast she can pay off her existing debt will play a significant role in the length of time it will take for her credit report to improve. This all may take Ariel many months; however, if she sticks to her commitment, pays off all revolving accounts, and keeps her accounts open and in good standing she will reap the benefits of good credit when she has accomplished this goal.

—Allen Humphris, RMCN general manager

Step 3: Correct Mistakes on Your Credit Report

Did you know? The Fair Credit Reporting Act requires credit reporting agencies to fix errors. Equifax says to check for charges you didn't make, inaccurate delinquencies, and accounts you didn't open. If you spot an error on your credit report, send a letter to each credit reporting agency to get it corrected.

Step 4: Don't Close Paid-Off (or Old) Accounts

Length of credit history: 15 percent of your credit score.

Did you know? Closing accounts doesn't help boost scores; it can sometimes hurt it. It's typically better to keep your accounts open, so your balance to credit limit ratio is better.

Closing your oldest accounts: Makes your credit history shorter.

"But, this happens only after the credit reporting agency removes the closed account record from your credit report, which usually happens only many years later," says Watts of Fair Isaac.

"FICO scores look at both your open and closed accounts on your credit report when assessing the length of your credit history."

Credit history: Shows how you've managed credit over time.

If you pay on time, keep your balances low and use credit wisely, your credit score will be affected positively, according to Freddie Mac.

If you keep low or zero balances on all your cards closing an account may affect you minimally.

Step 5: Avoid New Credit When Applying for a Mortgage

New credit: 10 percent of your credit score.

Credit Scenario #2: Meet Tom. He plans to buy a house in two years, with his brother co-signing. But, he has $10,000 in credit-card debt. The balance on his car is another $14,000 and he co-signed for his sister's car. His credit score is roughly 523. He wants to improve his credit so he can buy a house. What can he do?

RMCN'S Advice: Tom needs to make sure the payments on the car he co-signed for and his car are made on time every month. If at all possible, have his sister refinance the vehicle he co-signed in her name. To ensure his scores improve, I would also recommend paying off the credit card debt as soon as possible and keep the credit cards open. Also, a good healthy mix of good credit play a major role in a person's credit score. Once his credit card debt is paid, I would also recommend establishing one to two new credit accounts—unsecured would be best, secured if it is the only option.

—Allen Humphris, RMCN general manager

Tip: When you're about to apply for a loan, it is typically better not to apply for other new credit. Quicken Loans says if you open a lot of credit accounts in a short amount of time, it can represent a great risk. It can also lower your score. FICO score can usually distinguish between rate shopping and searching for many new credit accounts. (Requesting to check your credit report or score does not affect your score.)

Re-establishing your credit history: If you've had problems, MyFICO says, "Opening new accounts responsibly and paying them off on time will raise your score."

Step 6: Credit Counseling

Signs you need help: You can't make payments; you're behind on your bills, you have a lot of high-interest debt. Five warning signs you have too much debt:

1. The minimum is all you can pay on your credit card bills.
2. Your disposable income drops.
3. You max out your credit cards after paying off your balance.
4. You don't have emergency funds.
5. Unable to sleep at night.

Credit Scenario #3: Kelly bankrupted more than 10 years ago. She divorced her husband several years ago and hasn't been able to establish credit. She has two judgments (credit cards) and in the past year, got a secured card she always pays off. She hasn't been able to buy a car and would like to improve her credit so she can eventually buy a home. Where do you start?

RMCN'S Advice: "Kelly needs to keep her secured card below 20 percent of the limit at all times. To re-establish car credit it may be necessary to have a sizeable down payment at the time of purchase, between 20 percent and 30 percent of the sales price. Kelly may also receive a very high interest rate; probably upwards of 16 percent. Within 12 months of making her payments on time, keeping her credit card balance under 20 percent, and not having any new delinquencies added to her credit report she should be in a good position to refinance her vehicle. It would also be a good idea of establish one to two more revolving lines of credit for a healthy mix of accounts on her credit report."

—Allen Humphris, RMCN general manager

Where do you turn? Call your creditors to get help from a legitimate counselor. Non-profit counseling services can set up a repayment plan. They help negotiate lower interest rates and help you pay off your bills in a few years.

If you feel you need credit counseling: A reputable non-profit organization is Consumer Credit Counseling Service (CCCS). It provides free financial counseling, debt and money management, budget counseling, and more. You can make a face-to-face appointment at (800) 251-CCCS (2227). You can use the telephone or online counseling. Visit *www.cccsatl.org*.

Experts say that in the past, credit counseling could hurt your credit score if the counseling was noted on your credit report. But now, that's not true. Fair Isaac changed the FICO scoring formula in the late 1990s so that it now ignores any credit report references to credit counseling. After you finish your repayment plan, references to credit counseling is usually taken off your credit report.

Low Credit Score?

Quicken Loans shares common explanations for a lower credit score:

1. Serious delinquency: You have one for more accounts with late payments.
2. Serious delinquency and public record of collections filed: You have one or more accounts that have gone to a collection agency.
3. Time since delinquency is too recent or unknown: You have one or more accounts recently past due.
4. Amounts owed on accounts: Your amount of debt is too high relative to your credit limits.
5. Proportion of balances to credit limits on revolving accounts is too high: Balances on your credit cards are too high relative to your credit limits.
6. Length of time accounts have been established: The length of your credit history isn't long enough to show responsible credit management.
7. Too many accounts with balances: The number of accounts you have with balances raises concern over how much debt you're carrying.

Source: Quicken Loans

Considering bankruptcy? New laws say you must get government approved credit counseling within six months before filing for bankruptcy. For a state list of approved organizations, visit the U.S. Trustee Program within the U.S. Department of Justice at *www.usdoj.gov/ust*. Bankruptcy stays on your credit report for 10 years, hindering your ability to get credit, purchase a home, get insurance and, sometimes, a job. Those that do follow bankruptcy rules get a discharge that says they don't have to repay certain debts.

There are two types of bankruptcy:

1. Chapter 13: If you have steady income, it lets you keep property (house, car, boat) you'd otherwise lose in a bankruptcy. The court approves a 3- to 5-year repayment plan to pay off your debts rather than surrender your property.
2. Chapter 7: This bankruptcy is the sale of all assets (except those that may be exempt, such as work-related tools or basic household furnishings). You have to wait seven years before you can file Chapter 7 bankruptcy, whereas Chapter 13, you could file again in as little as two years.

Be wary of scams: Some ads offering debt relief may sometimes be offering bankruptcy. Check the company out with the Better Business Bureau or a local consumer protection agency. For more information, visit *www.ftc.gov/credit*.

Behind on Your Payments? Steps to Recovery

If you find yourself behind on your payments, Equifax recommends the following steps:

> **MONEY SAVERS:**
>
> Keep in mind, a low credit score can also affect your home and auto insurance.

- ✓ Start a budget. Analyze your spending habits.
- ✓ Avoid using your cards (but don't close them).

✓ Avoid getting new cards.

✓ Start paying off the account(s) with the highest interest rate first.

✓ Talk with your family about ways to cut expenses.

✓ Consider using some savings to pay off your debt (it could save you money in interest).

✓ Be wary of "credit repair" clinics that say they can remove bankruptcies or late payments. Source: Equifax

SHOESTRING TIP:

"The credit scores sold to consumers by Experian and TransUnion are not used by lenders and may be very different from the scores that lenders actually use. If consumers want to see the same score their lender uses, they need to learn their FICO scores, which are used by the overwhelming majority of U.S. businesses and lenders."

—Craig Watts, Fair Isaac

Getting Your Credit Score

While it is free to get a credit report every year from each main credit reporting agency, it does not come with a credit score. Most lenders will buy your credit score from Equifax, Experian, and TransUnion and then go with the middle score. Watts of Fair Isaac says, "Only mortgage lenders look at all three scores, because the consequences of bad credit decisions are so much greater in that field. For decisions about credit cards, auto loans, retail-store cards, and such, lenders generally use just one score from one CRA (credit reporting agency). But, since the consumer doesn't know which CRA will be tapped by the lender, we all should monitor our scores at all three CRAs."

To see your scores (there is a fee), you can contact each of the credit bureaus to see what score they have for you. We also have contacts for fraud alerts, how to dispute an item on your credit report, and more. This is their contact information:

⇨ Experian

www.experian.com

Order by phone, dispute an item on your report or report fraud: (888)-397-3742

⇨ Equifax

www.equifax.com

Order your report by phone: (800)-685-1111.

Fraud alert on your credit report: (888)-766-0008

Dispute an item on your credit report at *www.equifax.com.*

⇨ TransUnion

www.transunion.com

Free annual credit report: (877)-322-8228

Dispute an item on your credit report: (800)-916-8800 (or online)

Fraud Victim Assistance Department: (800)-680-7289

Order credit report, scores: *www.truecredit.com*

Free annual credit report: *www.annualcreditreport.com*

⇨ MyFICO

www.myfico.com

Identity Theft help

If you find you are a victim of identity theft, Quicken Loans recommends the following steps:

1. Contact the fraud departments at one of the credit bureaus. (We have previously provided those numbers.)
2. Close the accounts that have been used fraudulently or tampered with. Use the ID Theft Affidavit (*www.consumer.gov/idtheft/*) to dispute new unauthorized accounts.
3. File a police report.
4. File a complaint with the FTC because they have a database of ID theft cases used for investigations by law enforcement.

Q&A Credit Guidance

What credit scores receive the best interest rates? What are co-signing dangers? need tips for improving your credit? We talk with Fair Isaac, Co. (the folks behind the credit scoring system). Craig Watts shares insight with us:

Piper: Generally, what credit score receives the best interest rate?

Craig: That varies from lender to lender because different lenders have different risk tolerances, just as colleges have

Credit Scenario #4: Alex started with a credit score in the 700s. The three items on his credit report: His drool-worthy car, a bank credit card, and a credit card. When his brother asked him to co-sign a loan to consolidate his credit, Alex agreed. But, when his brother defaulted for 90 days, not paying the loan, it dropped Alex's pristine credit to the low 500s. He was devastated. He suddenly felt it would take years before he could improve his credit to buy a home.

RMCN'S Advice: The first thing Alex needs to do is make sure the loan is caught up to prevent further damage to his credit report. The next thing he needs to do is have his brother secure the loan in his name alone or pay off the loan entirely. Moving forward, Alex needs to make sure he pays his car and credit card on time and keep his credit card balance below 20 percent if at all possible. The other suggestions I have are to call the creditor, explain what happened, and ask them if there is anything they can do. Many creditors will remove the delinquent history if the account is kept current for six to 12 months; of course, this is not the case with all creditors. Make sure any agreement made verbally with the creditor is confirmed in writing from the creditor.

—Allen Humphris, RMCN general manager

different S.A.T. requirements for incoming freshmen. Speaking very generally, having a FICO score above the mid-700s (possible range is 300 to 850) should help qualify you for a lender's best rates.

Piper: If you co-sign a loan/credit card with someone and they fail to pay their bill and it lowers your credit score—how do you recover?

Craig: Delinquencies hurt FICO scores based on three criteria. Recency, severity (how many months it was delinquent), and frequency (how many other times does your credit report show a delinquency).

So, if your credit report shows a delinquent shared account, you should work with other(s) on that account to get it current as soon as you can. That will keep the severity from increasing. Recency is only helped by the passage of time. Frequency can be minimized by making sure no more accounts become delinquent in the future.

Piper: Is it true if you pay off certain items, it can help your score more than paying other items?

Craig: If you have seriously delinquent accounts on your credit report that are now in collections or have been charged off by the lender, you likely won't help your FICO score by paying off those delinquent accounts. The damage has already been done to your FICO score through the extent of the delinquency. Time alone will

SHOESTRING TIP:

New Credit Risk Score

There is a new kind of credit risk score that uses non-traditional credit information to predict the risk of consumers who don't yet have any credit account, credit cards, loans or other types of traditional credit. In a major lending-industry study, the FICO Expansion credit risk score was found to be a strong and reliable score for assessing the risk of millions who have no credit or little credit on file with Equifax, Experian, and TransUnion. Fair Isaac's FICO Expansion score is leading in this area.

—Watts, Fair Isaac.

help those accounts lessen their impact on your FICO score. As the accounts age, they will impact your score less.

Piper: When should you start looking at your credit report before deciding to buy? About how long does it take to improve your credit if it needs help?

Craig: For most people, checking their FICO scores six months before applying for a major loan will give them a good idea of their credit potential and allow them enough time to correct genuine errors on the credit report and pay down accounts with high balances, before approaching lenders with loan applications.

Facts & Fallacies

There are many facts and myths when it comes to credit. MyFICO says what is true and what is not when it comes to your credit.

- Fallacy: My score determines whether or not I get credit.
  Fact: Lenders use a number of facts to make credit decisions, including your FICO score. Lenders look at information such as the amount of debt you can reasonably handle given your income, your employment history, and your credit history. Based on their perception of this information, as well as their specific underwriting policies, lenders may extend credit to you although your score is low, or decline your request for credit although your score is high.

- Fallacy: A poor score will haunt me forever.
  Fact: Just the opposite is true. A score is a "snapshot" of your risk at a particular point in time. It changes as new information is added to your bank and credit bureau files. Scores change gradually as you change the way you handle credit. For example, past credit problems impact your score less as time passes. Lenders request a current score when you submit a credit application, so they have the

most recent information available. Therefore, by taking the time to improve your score, you can qualify for more favorable interest rates.

- Fallacy: Credit scoring is unfair to minorities.
  Fact: Scoring considers only credit-related information. Factors like gender, race, nationality, and marital status are not included. In fact, the Equal Credit Opportunity Act (ECOA) prohibits lenders from considering this type of information when issuing credit. Independent research has been done to make sure that credit scoring is not unfair to minorities or people with little credit history. Scoring has proven to be an accurate and consistent measure of repayment for all people who have some credit history. In other words, at a given score, non-minority and minority applicants are equally likely to pay as agreed.
- Fallacy: Credit scoring infringes on my privacy.
  Fact: Credit scoring evaluates the same information lenders already look at the credit bureau report, credit application and/or your bank file. A score is simply a numeric summary of that information. Lenders using scoring sometimes ask for less information (fewer questions on the application form, for example).
- Fallacy: My score will drop if I apply for new credit.

  Fact: If it does, it probably won't drop much. If you apply for several credit cards within a short period of time, multiple requests for your credit report information (called "inquiries") will appear on your report. Looking for new credit can equate with higher risk, but most credit scores are not affected by multiple inquiries from auto or mortgage lenders within a short period of time. Typically, these are treated as a single inquiry and will have little impact on the credit score.

Credit Scenario #5: John has excellent credit and low credit-card balances, is previously divorced paying child support, and lives in a townhome. What can he do to keep his pristine credit and does child support affect credit

RMCN'S Advice: John needs to keep doing exactly what he's been doing. He needs to be sure to keep his credit balances on his credit cards under 20 percent to 30 percent. As long as child support is being paid on time it rarely gets reported to the credit repositories. In the event that child support is deficient it is subjected to being reported as an adverse trade line. —Allen Humphris, RMCN general manager

Q & A: Did You Know?

Maxine Sweet, vice president of public education at Experian, gives us the inside scoop on how credit affects our loan options, how to build credit if you have no credit, and how to establishing good credit.

Piper: How does your credit history affect your loan options and interest rate?

Maxine: Lenders price their services according to risk. The higher your risk, the more likely you won't pay as agreed. So, if your credit history shows that you are an extremely low risk, you will pay lower down payment or whatever is appropriate for the type of transaction.

Piper: What is "ballpark" considered excellent, average, or poor credit?

Maxine: It varies by lender depending on the type of service. For some credit services, as long as your credit history is average or above, you will get the standard rate and if you are below average, you may be declined. In others, there are pricing levels. The Website, *www.nationalscoreindex.com,* contains information about the national average credit score, in addition to average credit scores in regions, states, and local areas. Consumers can also compare their debt level, late payments, and credit usage to others across the nation.

Piper: No credit? How do you build credit easily?

Maxine: There is no one simple way to establish credit for the first time, other than to accept a good revolving credit-card offer if it is made (usually when you are in college) and then use it wisely. More offers will follow. If you don't have that opportunity, try applying with the bank where you have your checking and/or savings account, get a secured card (where you deposit funds to offset the credit), or consider a joint application or asking your parents to co-sign. Be sure you understand the responsibilities associated with each type of account.

The first step in rebuilding your credit is to bring your delinquent accounts current and to reduce your existing debts. The most important thing is to always make all of your payments on time. Eventually, your credit history will show that you have regained control of your credit and have established good credit management practices. Then, you will be able to qualify for new credit when you need it.

Piper: Bankruptcy? How and when can you buy a home?

Maxine: It all depends on the lender. However, it would be safe to say that you are much more likely to pay a higher interest rate and/or higher down payment.

Piper: What are some tips for establishing good credit?

Maxine: The most simple and important tip is to always make your payments on time, whether you have one account or many. A consistent history of on-time payments is the strongest indicator that you are a good credit risk. An ideal credit history would have a mix of accounts, such as a car loan, mortgage, department store cards, and credit card—all managed well. However, you can have a very strong credit score with less.

It is particularly good to have a couple of credit cards because that is a better reflection of how you manage credit. You personally determine how much you will charge, how much you pay each month and how close to the limit you go. Also, the longer you have used credit, the more you have demonstrated that you can manage your finances. Consider that factor before closing old accounts.

Chapter 4

Finding a Great Realtor: Services Your Agent Should Provide

"Hire a Realtor to represent you. This is one of the most overlooked choices a buyer has. Get recommendations from friends, search the Internet, and so on. Then when you've narrowed down several choices, interview them. See which ones you feel comfortable with and, more importantly, which one truly wants to represent your best interests. Then, stick with them! If it's not working out fire them and hire another. It is much better than working with several agents at once (and more fair to the agent!)."

—Ron Roth, Principal, Premier Realty

Faye Brock is a Realtor folks love. Maybe it's her Southern hospitality that shines through on first encounter. But for certain, it's her vast knowledge of real estate that makes her the Realtor folks go to. She says to get an agent that is a knowledgeable buyer's agent, who has experience in the business. Faye says when you meet with the Realtor, after 30 to 40 minutes ask yourself if you think you would want to work together and if your personalities click.

Many Realtors are asking buyers to sign a buyer's agency agreement. Faye says if you sign a buyer's agency agreement, it's saying "Mr. Realtor will work for you for____days." She says if you aren't sure about the agent, ask them to only represent you two days or two weeks. Buyer's agency, Faye says, means "How long can we work together?"

Faye always tells her potential buyers, "You can have me for two days. I will work for you for two days and you'll come back to work with me for two years." Her clients always laugh, but it's true. Most of her business comes from referrals.

Faye, who has ranked in the top one percent nationwide in terms of real estate sales for 20 years for Century21, says it's important to look at a Realtor's past testimonials (track record with previous clients), their experience in the industry, and their education. For example, Faye has every certification and honor in her industry: ABR, CRS, GRI, RRS, and Broker/owner of Century 21 Brock & Associates in Wilmington, North Carolina. (See what these letters stand for behind your Realtor's name at the end of this chapter.)

Ultimately, when you select a Realtor, you want someone who is looking out for your best interests in the transaction, who finds a home that meets your needs, and guides you through the home-buying process with ease.

Finding a Realtor

There are millions of Realtors across the United States. How do you find the one to work for you? What is the difference between a buyer's agent or a seller's agent? Who pays the commission and what services should a Realtor offer you? We talk with real estate agent Leslie Nichols of RE/MAX Professional Group in Houston, Texas, for insight.

Piper: How do you find a Realtor?

Leslie: The best judge of a Realtor is their past clients. I would ask your friends/family for a referral and quiz them on why they liked them. If your friends/family don't have a good suggestion, you could look in the neighborhood in which you want to live and see who has the most signs or type that neighborhood into an online search and see who comes up. Then ask to meet with them and ask for a list of references from the agent. If they make you uncomfortable or don't have any references, run the other way.

> **SHOESTRING TIP:**
>
> You should see testimonials the Realtor has received from past clients. Just look at this testimonial Ron Roth received from Fox's *King of the Hill* associate producer!
>
> "Just a note of appreciation for the wonderful job you did in making my first home purchase a positive experience. Your patience and attentiveness in finding that perfect house with 'curb appeal' along with the effort and accessibility you gave through out the closing process (and beyond) was a great comfort."
>
> —Kenny Micka, Associate Producer, *King of the Hill*, Fox

Piper: What qualities and services should the Realtor provide you?

Leslie: They should be diligent in finding you a home that fits your needs, and they should not show you homes that are above the price you indicated you wanted to stay below. They should be ethical and professional at all times. They should give you their attention when they are with you and only answer their phone with your permission, because they are on your time. They should explain local customs that will affect you (such as property taxes). They should walk you through the necessary steps and keep you on track with the process and they themselves should understand the process. They should be available at reasonable times to answer your questions. They should negotiate with your best interest in mind, not their own. They should have referrals of service providers to work with but should not require you to use them. Excluding Intermediary, they should provide you with advice and a market analysis based on comparable sales. They should attend the closing. If you want to have a lifelong relationship with your Realtor (this is our goal), they should be available for questions that come up along the years. They should help your referrals to them the same way they helped you.

> **Hot Tip:**
>
> **How do you select a good Realtor?**
>
> "Be sure they have bought and sold their own property as they'll better understand the emotions that occur through the process. Also be sure they are very experienced and have been in the business at minimum a few years. See their track record and call a customer they helped to see how they rated."
>
> —Laura Denise Milkowski, Vice President
> The LDM Team at Corcoran in New York

Piper: For first-time homebuyers, please describe the difference between buyer's agent and seller's agent. With buyer's agents, who pays the commission?

Leslie: A buyer's agent works for the buyer only. A seller's agent works for the seller only. In our area, we also have Intermediaries. An Intermediary could be the same agent servicing the seller and the buyer or it could be different agents from the same brokerage. An Intermediary Relationship requires both the buyer's and seller's written permission, and both the Buyer Representation Agreement and Listing Agreement must authorize the Intermediary Relationship as well. These ensure the buyer and seller are represented equally. Basically an agent working in an Intermediary position, needs to treat everyone fairly and cannot disclose information to either party that may give one the upper hand. The builder or seller pays the commission, unless they refuse, in which case the buyer would pay. We have never had anyone refuse to pay us. We have even sold For Sale By Owner (FSBO) homes and were paid our commission at closing. One scenario on a FSBO home: the asking price was $35,000 higher than the highest comparable sold. Our clients got the home at their first offer, which was $35,000 less than the asking price. The seller said, "You guys really did your homework." We really did.

Piper: What are the reasons why you should use a buyer's agent?

Hot Tip:

If you need to find a Realtor, *Realtor.com* has a great search engine for finding an agent in your area. You can type in your city and state. Instantly, it pulls up a listing of available Realtors with their phone numbers, Websites, available listings, and you can even zip them an e-mail.

Leslie: You should use a buyer's agent with resale *and* new homes. The seller or builder pays the buyer's agent. In our area, the builder charges the buyer the same price whether they use an agent or not, so it is a free service to the buyer. You should use a buyer's agent because you have a professional in your corner working in your best interests. If you buy a new home, the sales counselor works for the builder not the buyer, and they are not licensed by your local real estate commission as your agent is. Agents understand the process and can walk the home buyer through the steps and keep them updated throughout the process as well as let them know if what is happening is normal and customary or out of the ordinary.

Hot Tip:

If you are relocating from one city to another, it is always a good idea to look for an agent who specializes in relocation to help you. RE/MAX Real Estate Services Broker Stephen O' Hara in San Juan Capistano, California, created an interesting relocation site for parents, *www.parentrelocationcouncil.org*. (It also has interesting stats, demographics, information for each of the states.)

Piper: You find the house of your dreams. Do you use the selling agent as your agent, too? What are the pros and cons of that situation?

Leslie: I believe that most surveys say that buyers choose the first agent they talk to. If this is the case, then most of the time you would presume that the buyer is in fact contacting the listing agent of the first property they want to see. Also, most buyers do not buy the first house they see, but then go out and view all available homes that match their criteria.

If you do find the house of your dreams, and it happens to be with the listing agent, it could be smooth sailing or it could be a disaster. In our area, we call this Intermediary Relationship. We have sold several of our own listings, and everyone was very happy with the outcome. For these purposes, we will assume that the agent in question is an experienced, caring professional, which is a must for this to work. Pros: faster communications, able to keep the sale together. Cons: None.

If the home is priced right (per the comparable sales) and with the seller's permission, giving the buyer a market analysis is not contradictory to the seller's goals, thus I can supply it. If, however, the home is overpriced, I cannot give a market analysis to the buyer, unless the seller allows me to do so and explain why the home is so much better than the comparables.

Example of this situation: Once we took a listing that had been on the market a year with another agent. We took the listing on a Saturday, the owners had some prep work to do and it would be a few days before we got it into MLS (Multiple Listing Service, a list of homes that are for sale). We had been working with a couple for a few weeks that we felt would be perfect buyers. On Sunday, we showed them 14 homes—this one being the first one. We wrote a contract on this house on Tuesday. The seller ended up giving an allowance for the items they were going to do (paint, dishwasher, and oven)—and both the buyers and sellers preferred it that way. We closed in 3 to 4 weeks from contract with a trusted lender and we funded our closing date. All were happy!

In this sale, the home was in above-average condition and priced just right. The buyer was pre-approved and both buyers and sellers were motivated and realistic. Intermediary Relationships would not work if all of these conditions were not met.

Insiders Insight

What is your number one no-no?:

"Not interviewing and hiring an agent to represent your best interest. This to me is the number-one no-no! A lot of buyers will just work with the first agent they come into contact with, whether it is from an open house, a sign call, or an ad call. The number-two no-no would be working with the listing agent (agent representing the seller) to buy the home. This is called 'dual agency' (this is not permitted in some states). Some buyers feel that they can get a better deal this way because the agent can (but not always) reduce their commission and get a lower price. Some buyers also feel that because the agent knows the seller it may be an easier transaction. Usually the opposite is true. Remember that the agent owes a fiduciary duty to the seller. They owe you nothing but "honesty" and fair dealing, or, better put, you are on a lower level and there is no way that the agent can fight for you.

"Here is an analogy I like to use. If you were about to go on trial would you just go up to the prosecutor and try to work a deal or would you go out and hire the best defense possible?"

"Note: In most all circumstances the commission is paid by the seller. The buyer does not pay a penny for the representation of a buyer's agent"

—Ron Roth, Principal, Premiere Realty, California

Piper: Is there other advice you would like to add?

Leslie: Sometimes agents take days off and even take vacations. We have to relax and refresh so we can be our best for ourselves and our clients. Would you want to work with a doctor who works seven days a week and answers their phone in the middle of surgery? A professional experienced agent most likely will have appointments scheduled out for several days, so be patient if you cannot get the first appointment you want. Rookie agents have tons of time on their hands. Who do you want to help you buy a home? An experienced agent is well worth waiting a day or two to see.

You need to decide if you prefer to have a one-person Realtor or a team. Teams are becoming more popular among Realtors. Sometimes there could be missed communication if the team is too big. You should select a full-time Realtor. If they cannot commit to being a Realtor full time, why would you commit to them?

Check Credentials: Learn the Real Estate ABCs

> "A strong real estate agent takes our business seriously and is continually working on increasing his or her knowledge base and keeping abreast of industry trends and developments. Here are some of my memberships, affiliations, and accreditations and what they mean. Make sure your agent has at least a few of these, too."
>
> —Faye Brock, ABR, CRS, GRI, RRS and Broker/Owner for Century21 Brock & Associates in Wilmington, NC

CRS: Only four percent of Realtors have CRS credentials. This is the most rigorous and professional residential designation available to Realtors: Consider it the Ivy League university of residential real estate. The Certified Residential Specialist (CRS) designation recognizes professional accomplishments in both experience and education. The CRS program is open to Realtors who want to keep abreast of the latest sales and marketing techniques, enhance their professionalism, and increase their earning power.

Realtor: All Realtors are licensed to sell real estate as an agent or a broker but not all real estate agents are Realtors. Only Realtors can display the REALTOR® logo. Realtors belong to the National Association of Realtors (NAR) and pledge to follow the Code of Ethics, a comprehensive list containing 17 articles and underlying standards of practice, which establish levels of conduct that are higher than ordinary business practices or those required by law. Less than half of all licensees are Realtors®.

ABR: (Accredited Buyer Representative) is a designation from the Real Estate Buyer's Agent Council that trains experienced Realtors in specifically representing the real estate consumer. The ABR designation is awarded to real estate practitioners who complete a comprehensive two-day REBAC course in buyer representation, achieve a passing grade on the written examination, and demonstrate practical experience by completing and closing five real estate transactions in which the candidate functioned as a buyer's representative. ABRs must also maintain a membership in good standing with the National Association of Realtors and the Real Estate Buyer's Agent Council.

GRI: (Graduate, REALTOR® Institute) The GRI designation is earned by completing a national program of specialized and advanced education for the licensed Realtor. It involves intense study, covering many special aspects of real estate such as residential marketing, cost basis, appreciation methods, investment real estate, construction, real estate tax concepts, exchanges, capital gains, and various types of mortgage programs. This designation may only be earned after successfully completing a rigorous educational program that requires 92 hours of live coursework.

Broker: A real estate broker is a party who acts as an intermediary between sellers and buyers of real estate. Real estate brokers and their salespersons (commonly called "real estate agents") assist sellers in marketing their property and selling it for the highest possible price under the best terms. When acting as a buyer's agent with a signed agreement, they assist buyers by helping them purchase property for the best possible price under the best terms. Without an agreement, brokers may assist buyers in the acquisition of property but still represent the seller and the seller's interests. All brokers can act as real estate agents; not all agents are brokers. Make sure you find out exactly what your agent will do and what the agent will have other people doing on his or her behalf.

Source: *FayeBrock.com*

Chapter 5

Smart House-Hunting
Finding Your Dream Home
(At the Price You Want)

You know you want a house.

But, what do you want?

After you know how much you can afford (and how much you actually want to spend), it becomes a matter of what you're looking for in a house. You will be the one writing that check every month. You'll want to pull your car into the driveway and say, "That is my house. And, I love it so much." Just remember, it will be coming out of your pocket (for years...cough, cough). A long-term commitment of sorts, so don't rush, there is time to find what you want. Old-fashioned advice: "Go with your gut instinct." And as my good friend told me, "Don't buy if there is anything at all that bothers you about it." We're here to give you tips on how to shop smart.

Lana Jo Matthis had been living in her home for 28 long years with her husband. Both retired, they wanted a home that would fit their needs at this new stage in their life. After nine months to a year, they finally found a nice family home: four bedrooms, 3 1/2 bathrooms, a large entry with a beautiful stairway, 3 1/2-car garage, and a gorgeous courtyard Lana Jo can see from her dream kitchen. While it was a little bigger than they wanted (and it came with a pool they didn't need)—they fell in love with the home and knew it had to be theirs. When you ask if the wait and long search was worth it, there is a resounding "yes." They admit they probably drove their Realtor, Bob Nichols, crazy, but they only have kind words to say about how wonderful he was in taking the time to show them new homes until they finally found "the one."

"It all came together with this house," says Lana Jo. "There are enough houses on the market to find what you want."

According to statistics, there are six million homes sold every year. Just visit *www.Realtor.com*, run by the National Association of Realtors. It is, by far, the largest listing of homes for sale across the country. Co-owner/broker associate for ReMax Cherry Creek, Inc., in Denver, Colorado, Jim Thoeming says, "Buy in the best location that you can for the long term in the home's appreciation and in terms of your enjoyment of the house."

When you are deciding what you want in a home, what are you looking for? The key factors are price, location, square footage, and amenities (new appliances, pool, and so on). But, the other factor to consider is your lifestyle: How long will you be living in the home? Is your family growing? Are you retiring? What schools are in the area? What is important to you in terms of location, price, desirable features, or lifestyle? Realtor Craig Harrison of Twin Tower Realty in Richmond, Virginia, says, "Tell your Realtor what you are looking for in a home and what your needs/situation is so they can best find what works for you."

Broker Sherri Strickland of Cornerstone Properties in Texas says, "For instance, don't just tell your agent: 'I want a three-bedroom, two-bath home priced in the low $100,000s.' Give your agent as much information as possible about what you are looking for to suite your needs/wants in a home. This will keep you from being shown homes that you would never consider for one reason or another and you won't wear your agent out either!"

What are you looking for in a home?

- Price range.
- Monthly payment you feel comfortable with.
- Location(s) you want to live in.
- Square footage.
- Amenities.
- What you really want in a house.
- What you are looking for long term.

SHOESTRING TIP:

"The key is to sit down and make some decisions about your personal house goals: location, purpose (are you downsizing/ upsizing), and cost/pricing. Write down as many of your goals that you want to accomplish. For the buying process, include your time frame. For selling, include your time to commit to the process. It's best to have an overall strategy and personal goals. The sooner you meet with a Realtor to fine tune your goals, the more quickly you can achieve them."

"You put your faith in your doctor and lawyer, as with any other professional you would consult. Put your faith in your Realtor and listen to their advice."

—Tom Stevens, National Association of Realtors

Starting the Search

When Sherri Strickland sits down with her buyers for the first time, the very first thing they talk about is financing. She asks: "How much do you want to put down? What are you comfortable with paying monthly?" She sends them to a lender to get pre-qualified or pre-approved (see Chapter 2) to make sure they can buy a home at the current time or to find out when they can buy. (Some Realtors recommend finding a Realtor first that can then help direct you toward a lender.)

The broker at Cornerstone Properties in Victoria, Texas, also has her clients sign a Buyer's Representation Agreement saying she is their real estate agent who will help and educate them in their home-buying process. From there, the process of finding a home gets rolling.

Hot Tip:

What is your best tip for smart house-hunting?

"Establish a relationship with a qualified agent for personal education and updated information. Then, have the agent set up your criteria for a home on an automatic contact basis through their computerized MLS system and *trust* the agent in what they can do for you."

—Larry Melichar, president and CEO, CBSHome Real Estate in Omaha, Nebraska

Effective Home-Searching Tactics

You've scoured newspaper ads, online sites, open houses, and you've glanced at the list your Realtor gave you of homes for sale. We all know how to find a home, but what should we be looking for once we walk in the door. What should be red flags? When home buyers walk through a home for the first time, they pay attention to the paint, carpet, or other minor details. We are never trained to look for the major items we should pay attention to. So, I asked home inspector Reggie Marston, who has looked at countless homes: "What are key areas you should pay attention to?"

"Just pay attention to your surroundings. Your senses are normally your best indicator of possible major issues," says Reggie, president of the Northern Virginia Chapter of ASHI and owner of Residential Equity Management Home Inspections. "As you walk around the exterior, look for things that just don't seem right or out of place."

As you walk around the house upon first inspection, Reggie has these tips for alerting your eyes to a few key areas inside and outside in his own words:

Outside the home:

- Look for excess of roofing shingle granules lying at the end of the downspouts. May need a new roof. Look for large cracks in the foundation—1/8-inch or more.
- Possible structural issues. Look at the slope of dirt away from the foundation. Possible basement water issues. Make notes on what you've seen on the exterior and move inside.

Inside the home:

- When you walk inside stop and smell. Does the house smell musty or moldy? There may be water leakage problems.
- Are the floors level, do you sense that you are walking uphill or downhill as you go through various rooms? Are there any large cracks in the walls? Possible structural issues.
- Go through the house and listen. Is the heating system excessively loud? Does it squeal, grind, or rattle? Does the air conditioner make any unusual noises? Possible HVAC issues.
- Flush the toilets and run the water in the sinks. Does the water sound like it continues to run in the toilet longer than normal? When you run water through the faucets, does the water appear to have good flow? Does the water look clear or does it look cloudy, rusty, or dirty? Does the water squeal loudly coming through the faucet or shower head? When you shut the faucets off, does it make a loud banging noise or vibrate the pipes? Possible plumbing issues.

- When looking at the electric service panel, does it have fuses or circuit breakers? Does the panel appear old or too small for the home? A half dozen fuses or breakers may indicate that the electric system may not have been updated. Do any of the switches feel hot? Standing close to the electric service panel, do any of the breakers or fuses buzz or hum loudly, are there switches that don't seem to operate anything, are there a lot of extension cords being used? Do any receptacles feel hot? Possible electric issues.

Reggie says, "Chances are if it doesn't seem right, it probably isn't."

Insiders Insight

What are small problems that can turn into future nightmares and how do you spot them? "Normally problems associated with health, safety, or monetary issues. For instance, take a loose electric receptacle, it's an aggravation that when you plug a light or a device into the receptacle, you have to wiggle the plug a little to get it to work. It works, the light turns on, but the receptacle is overheating because of the poor electrical contact and then can start a fire that could burn the house down. Small problem, huge nightmare. Another problem that I encounter regularly is that most homeowners don't service their HVAC systems or humidifiers as regularly as they should. Over a period of time algae, mold, and numerous other allergens as well as dust and dirt can build up in the system and cause respiratory problems, allergies, and even illnesses as serious as legionnaires disease."

—Reggie

(Later on in the process, you will have an experienced home inspector that should be critical in uncovering these types of problems that if left unrepaired can lead to much larger problems later and should be checked by a professional.)

New Technology

There is new technology that makes the home-buying search more interactive and fun. I asked

National Association of Realtors former president Tom Stevens to share with us some of the newest online applications for home searches. This is what he said about new online features:

- Virtual commercials: Videos about the home that include narration and soundtrack. High definition zoom: Tool that lets buyers focus in on specific details, such as crown moldings and architectural features.
- Satellite images: Aerial photos that show the home as well as its neighborhood surroundings.
- Interactive floor plans: Applications in which buyers can rearrange existing floor plans to see if their furniture would work in the space.

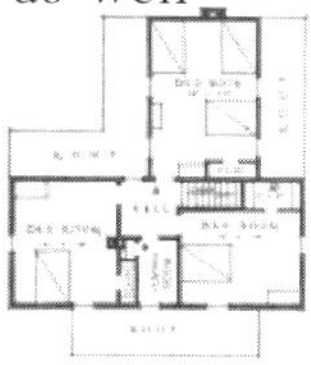

"New applications are also streamlining the mortgage application and settlement process," says Tom. "Automatic underwriting now allows mortgage applicants to be approved in a fraction of the time it used to take. Transaction management software helps Realtors manage the complex process from contract acceptance through inspections and contingency deadlines to closing."

He says, "Technology can certainly facilitate the home-buying process, but in real estate, high tech doesn't come at the expense of high touch."

> **SHOESTRING TIP:**
>
> "When surveyed, only 40 percent of recent buyers believe technology skills are very important in selecting a real estate agent. In contrast, 80 to 90 perfcent of home buyers ranked people skills, negotiation skills, responsiveness, and knowledge of the purchase process as very important."
>
> —Tom Stevens, National Association of Realtors

Common Mistakes to Avoid

"What are the most common mistakes you see buyers make?" I asked Jim Thoeming, when I finally caught up with him. A hard man to reach because he's always on the go showing houses or spending time with his family. He is highly regarded by his peers as an expert. The co-owner/broker associate of ReMax Cherry Creek, Inc. in Denver, Colorado, thought a moment and then shared the mistakes we can avoid:

- Reacting emotionally to a home. He says many times  buyers react to the paint, curtains, carpet—inexpensive features in relation to the home's structure and location. Also, he says, buyers should be aware of the community before committing to a home.
- Getting into a wrong loan program for your situation. For 

example, say you're buying as a single person or a couple and you know your income will be the same for the next few years. But, say the loan you selected will increase after a few years—and you will have to pay more than you can afford, giving you no choice but to sell the home.
- Haven't thought through the whole home-owning process:  Have you thought about the maintenance part of owning a home? Do you want to cut grass, plant flowers, and rake leaves? Would a condo or town home work better for you?
- Reacting to a house because it's cute rather than if it's well priced.
- It's important to understand your limitations on time, money and skill. If you don't have the time or money work on a home that needs to be fixed up, don't buy a home that needs to be fixed up.
- Bite off more than you can chew. Just because you can qualify for the loan, does it mean you want to spend that much?

MONEY SAVERS:

"Everyone is on a budget so it is important to understand what you are getting into. You must feel comfortable with your monthly payments. You also must assume you are going to have unexpected expenses arise. If you have a yard you must be able to maintain it. You must also be comfortable maintaining the structure. It is important that you are willing to make changes in your lifestyle—you are investing in your future. This may mean you have to eat more meals at home, take less time off, take on a second job, not go on vacation or buy a new car. Whatever you must do to get into your first home, you must do. You are investing in your future!"

—Clinton Wade, Estate Agent, President's Circle,
Prudential California Realty, Pacific Design Center,
West Hollywood, California

Checklist: Important Questions to Ask

When Sheng Li was purchasing his first home in Texas, he had a list of concerns that went through his mind, and it's a list of considerations to take into account when buying:

- ☑ Questions about the location of the home: Is it safe? Is there easy access to major highways, shopping, entertainment, and what is the proximity to your workplace? What events are held around the location, the potential for future growth, and appreciation?
- ☑ Neighborhood: How many homes are there in the neighborhood? What type of people live around this house, owner/renter ratio and demographics?
- ☑ House itself: What is the square footage, age, condition, and are there any major/minor problems?
- ☑ Previous owner: Why do they want to move and what is the flexibility of terms?
- ☑ Pricing: Is the price fair, what are the prices of similar houses around it, and what is trend of the price over the years?

Hot Tip:

What is the best way to investigate the safety of an area (crime stats), upcoming developments, schools, and so on. What is the best way to research an area before buying?

"The National Association of Realtors directs sales agents to only suggest clients go to appropriate Websites and let them interpret the information regarding crime statistics, (sexual offenders), etc. Most cities and municipalities have maps, addresses, pictures of the individuals, and more. School districts also have wonderfully informative sites. Often just going to a city site there are links to schools, cultural venues (museums, symphony, theater), sports, hospitals (including teaching universities) and much, much, more. An excellent source for governmental information (new roads, subdivisions, projects involving eminent domain) can be obtained on the specific links to city or county sites and more specifically to 'planning and zoning, or development.'"

—Roberta Alford, Coldwell Banker Gundaker,
St. Louis, Missouri

☑ Other costs: What is the closing cost and process? "You have to think about when you go to resell. It's all about investment. Buying a house is probably one of the biggest investments people make," says Faye Brock, broker/owner of Century 21 Brock and Associates.

Faye recommends the following important questions to ask before selecting your home:

☑ How long before appreciation goes back up?

☑ How much would the homeowners insurance be on the property?

☑ When was the last time the city/county did a tax evaluation? (If they do one right after you move in, evaluations go up and taxes go up.)

- ☑ Is the property in a city and the county? If it's in both, watch out for double taxation.
- ☑ Does the property have county water and sewer, or is it well and septic? If you are using a government loan to purchase a home (say an FHA or VA loan) you will need to get your septic/water inspected—an expense added to closing costs.
- ☑ Is the area close to water/marshland; you may need flood insurance? Will you able to afford the insurance?

Hot Tip:

How do you know if it's in a flood area?

Flood elevation is required by lenders. The only person who does this is a surveyor and he gives you flood certification; from there you would find out how much flood insurance you would need.

—Faye Brock

MONEY SAVER:

Unexpected expenses to consider:

"Some unexpected homeowner expenses to consider are things like yard maintenance, homeowner dues (condo), repairs (roof/plumbing/electrical), assessments (if you are purchasing a condo). With a condo it is always good to find out how much money the Home Owners Association has in reserves. This will help you understand the likelihood of an assessment. The less they have in reserves the more likely an assessment is."

—Clinton Wade, Estate Agent, President's Circle, Prudential California Realty, Pacific Design Center, West Hollywood, California

Chapter 6

Js That House Worth That Price?

The seller wanted $185,000.

It was at least $20,000 overpriced compared to similar homes for sale in the neighborhood. A few weeks passed. The priced dropped to $175,000. It was still $10,000 to high. After looking at comparable market analyses from their Realtor of what other area homes sold for, the buyers knew the house should really be going for $165,000. Finding out the sellers were in a financial pinch and needing help with closing costs as buyers, they negotiated.

Negotiating is an art. Knowing if a home is overpriced or underpriced is essential to your negotiations. When you resell a few years from now, you want to get a turnover on your investment. So, you don't want to overpay now. In this chapter, we cover how to tell if a house is worth that price, incentives sellers can offer you to buy, and more.

How Do J Know Jf the Price Js Right?

Say you find a home you fall in love with. It's $255,000. How can you tell if that is a good price for the house? That is where your Realtor's skills come in. You want a Realtor that can do a very good "comparable market analysis" (CMA), which lets you know how much similar homes sold for recently, how long it took to sell, and the asking price of homes currently on the market. A CMA gives you all the nitty-gritty details, including: maximum, minimum, and average selling prices for the area, as well as price per square foot.

For example, say the average price per square foot was $100, the selling price for a 2,000-square-foot home would be $200,000. If the lowest price per square foot was $78, the price would be $156,000. "The key thing is a real estate agent who knows how to do a proper market analysis," says real estate agent Larry Wallenstein of Re/Max Consultants Realty in Fort Lauderdale, Florida. And honestly, after spending months of looking at homes and prices, home buyers tend to be in tune with whether a home is overpriced, underpriced, or just right.

There are also other factors that affect pricing:

- Location: When you are looking for a home, location is the most important part. "First of all, buy in the best location that you can; it's the smartest thing you can do in the long-term in terms of the home's appreciation and your enjoyment of the house," says Jim Thoeming, associate broker/co-owner of Re/Max Cherry Creek in Denver. As he explained, there was an area that was developed with new homes in Colorado that had never had homes in that area before, but when the housing market took a turn, folks in that area were unable to sell. Areas that had a track record of being in a strong location (selling well) continued to sell. As he said, sometimes if you pick a good location—just the land you are on itself is what is wanted. When you look at an area, notice its economic stability, schools, local government, and property taxes (property taxes may be higher in one area than another nearby location). Above all else, make sure you select a home that has good resale potential.
- Property condition: How well is the home maintained? Is the inside well taken care of or does it look like a lot of work needs to be done?

MONEY SAVER:

You're on a shoestring budget—what are ways you can cut costs/save money when buying?

"Many people think that buying a cheap home will save them money. Often they resort to a home in poor condition or a manufactured home in hopes of saving money. Although it is sometimes a good strategy, it more often puts the buyers in dire straights. Trying to buy cheaply can jeopardize your dreams of home ownership and eventually your credit. Here is why:"

"If you are short on funds, buying a home in poor condition is extremely risky. Once you get into the home, where do get the funds for repairing/remodeling? If you are not able to do the repairs, will you have to walk away and let the home be foreclosed?"

—Kathi Frank, RE/MAX
The Woodlands and Spring

- How quickly are homes selling? When you look at the comparable market analysis with your Realtor, pay attention to how long it is taking homes to sell in the area in which you're interested. For example, you notice homes are selling quickly in the area—chances are it is a seller's market, where the ball is in their court. There are more buyers competing for fewer homes, meaning the sellers will tend to get asking price (or close to it or higher). In a buyer's market, you will see homes lingering for sale for longer periods of time, meaning there are fewer buyers and many sellers. In this market, that means the ball is in your court, where you have more of a chance of asking for seller concessions (like asking the seller to help you with closing costs, if needed).
- What is the seller's motivation? It's important to know the seller's motivation for selling. I will share two scenarios with you and why it's important.

Scenario #1: Aaron really wanted this two-story colonial in a very prime area of the suburbs. They have good resale prices, the home was in impeccable conditionm, and the price was really good, almost a steal. The sellers weren't in a rush to sell. They were testing the water to see how much they could get for their house. After they started searching for a home, they found out that they couldn't afford a better home than the one they were currently in, and, ultimately, this deal never worked. The seller decided they didn't want to sell and they made negotiations so difficult, the buyer decided not to buy.

Scenario #2: This seller owned a gas station and bought a new house to be closer to work. The house he was trying to sell was more than an hour away. He needed and wanted to sell desperately. The buyer knew a couple of things:

1. The seller had told them he really needed to sell. (Tip for sellers: Never tell buyers your desperation to sell.)
2. The buyers knew they needed help with closing costs. The buyers knew the ball was in their court. The buyers asked the seller for help with closing costs, they asked the seller to take care of a number of repairs, and they got the house at a price they were comfortable with. Knowing the seller's motivation is everything.

- Your motivation for buying: I will give you the same tip I just gave sellers: Don't let the seller know your love of the house. You want the ball to be in your court. But for you, how much time do you have to find a home you love? Do you have a lot of time or do you need to move quickly? Buying and selling is almost a will of wants. Do you need to move into town quickly, compared to the seller who has time to test the water? Or does the seller really need to sell because he has two mortgages from buying one home before selling? Understand everyone's needs, timeframes, and work together to have the best outcome for everyone.
- Hot selling seasons: The best times for house sales are the spring and fall. That is when the most homes tend to be for sale.

(Winter tends to be a slow season and real estate gurus notice that homes tend to sell for lower prices during this time.)

Doing Your Research

Aside from comparable market analysis' from your Realtor which is genuinely your best tool for seeing if a home is priced right, there are other ways you can get a feel for housing prices in the areas you are interested in:

- County assessor's Website or office: Want to know what your neighbor's house sold for? Check out this site. This public information is available to everyone. This is the same information Realtors use in a CMA, but software makes it easier for them to pull this information. Some Realtors will tell you how they used to go down to the county assessor's office to get this information, now technology has made it so easy.
- Open houses: Visit open houses in the area(s) you are interested in buying. Check out newspaper ads, real estate magazine/pamphlets, for sale signs, and pick up fliers at those homes you like when you drive-by. Get a grassroots pulse for the market.
- Online and private companies: You can get CMAs or see what prices area homes are selling for online. (Visit *Zillow.com*). There are also sights that will let you submit what you are looking for in a home and Realtors will respond to you. (Visit *Homegain.com* or Yahoo! Real Estate.) The list goes on and on. *Realtor.com* is the Multiple Listing Service online, where you can see all the homes that are for sale. At one time, Realtors were afraid of the MLS being online, but it's only become a great tool for buyers.

What Is a Seller Concession?

Let's see...It's like going to McDonald's and getting the happy meal (comes with a toy), or when you buy one pair of shoes and get the other at half price. It's an incentive. So, when it comes to selling homes (and particularly in a buyer's market or if homes are slow to sell), sellers will start offering things so you buy their home.

Closing cost help: If you need help with closing costs—let the sellers know up front. A mortgage officer will be able to help with this aspect (where the sales price can be bumped up to cover some of the closing costs for you but not get the lender in trouble).

MONEY SAVER:

"Be aware of your market place; shop and compare, get a sense for what properties have to offer. Calculate true costs before and after taxes; consult with your accountant. One should be able to negotiate with the seller and not be afraid to ask for things even though they may sound unusual; that is, paying for closing costs, rate buy-downs, upgrades to the property, etc. I have financed many strange deals that have made me say 'WOW! How'd they do that?' The most common answer I get from my client is; 'All I did was ask for it.'"

—Alex Elezai, Private Mortgage Banker, Countrywide

Home warranty: It is becoming more and more commonplace to ask for a one-year home warranty. (I definitely recommend you ask for one.) A home warranty policy covers unexpected repairs in the home. Home warranties cost several hundred dollars (many times $300 to $400).

Pre-inspection: A savvy seller will do a pre-inspection before putting their house on the market. The pre-inspection gives a seller a chance to tell buyers up front what is wrong with the home (and if they made the repairs after finding out). But, as a buyer, it is always recommended—even if the seller did a prè-inspection—that you have your own inspection done on the house.

Decorating allowance: Here is an example. A Realtor was selling a rancher with good square footage and clean curb appeal. When he got feedback from other Realtors who were showing the house, the comment he kept getting: "Oh, that carpet!" It was a shag-like carpet with multicolor that no matter how much people liked the house, they simply could not get over the carpet. So, as an incentive, they offered buyers $1,000 to go toward carpet. The house, with its hideous carpet, sold. There are a lot of creative incentives Realtors come up with to sell their homes. For example, paint allowances when they know the paint in the home has seen better days and other creative ideas.

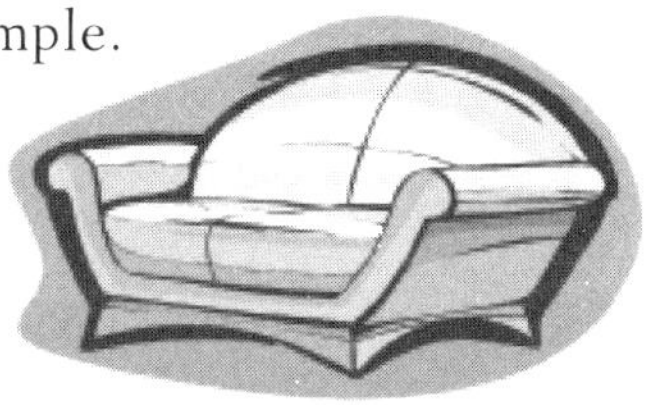

Amenities and conveyances: Sometimes a home will have great amenities such as marble countertops and stainless steel appliances. It is normal for buyers to ask for some items to "convey" such as the stove, refrigerator, washer, dryer, and so on. There are also those few unusual requests, such as the drapes, the carpet in the living room, or chandeliers. What is the worst they can say: "No." Just ask, if it's a yes, it's a yes.

Flexible about closing date and move-in arrangements: Buyers and sellers who express flexible closing date and move-in arrangements are always an incentive.

Other Factors to Consider

It can be wonderful and stressful to search for a new place to live. There are so many factors to consider: Where do you want to live, the suburbs or the city? What do you think about the architecture, landscaping, and amenities? Is it worth the price? Fair market value takes into consideration direct and indirect factors you will be thinking about, too.

MONEY SAVER:

Closing Tactics to Save You Money

"It is good to look at the timing. Say for example you lease an apartment on August 1st. In addition to August rental you have the deposit expense. Then on September 1st you have another month's rent to pay. If you close on the purchase of your home on August 1st, the first house payment will not be due until October 1st...and that is quite a bonus when it all comes together!" says Kathi Frank, Re/Max The Woodlands and Spring. For more on closing tactics and ways to save you money when buying visit Chapter 7.

Direct Factors on Fair Market Value

- Community: Is it close to shopping centers, area services, conveniences, and is there overall desirability of location?
- Zoning and planning: Ask your Realtor if there are future developments expected in the area. Community development plans can be positive or negative. Also Ask your Realtor about the history of the land your home is built on
- Schools: Good schools can be very important. Many times folks with children list this as one of the top priorities for moving to an area.
- Transportation: Is your home close to the highway or does it have easy access to transportation?
- Neighborhood: Is the neighborhood in a good location, attractive, and safe? Some experts say to buy a home that is more in the center of the neighborhood and to try avoid the homes that are at the entrance or near busy roadways, so that when you go to resell, it's easier to sell your home. Are homes selling well in the area? Is it taking them a long or short time to sell? Are the neighbors nice, are their yards well kept, and is the overall location good.

Indirect Factors on Fair Market Value

There are also factors that no one can control that affects fair market value.

- Disaster: Natural disasters, such as earthquakes, wildfires, hurricanes, tornados, and so on, can lower prices, especially if this is something that is reoccurring. (Hot tip: For example, if you are moving into an area that gets hit by hurricanes every year, ask your Realtor what kind of insurance you would need, so you can look into insurance costs before moving there, too).
- Economic changes: If the economy is good, home prices increase and there is a rise in sales. But, if it's a depressed economy, then home prices decrease and sales are less. Economy is very individual for your particular area as well.
- Demographic changes: How is the area changing? What are the demographics of your area?

Insiders Insight

How do you tell if a home is priced just right—or not?

"Pricing a home is the most difficult thing a Realtor does! SOLDs are history. The price we use today is for today's market, not yesterday's. In analyzing current data it is more important to look at active listings, pending sales, and factor in number of days on market along with trends that show a balanced market, buyer's advantage or seller's advantage market. Seller's should discount national media reporting because every city and subdivision is unique. It is not possible to compare apples and oranges! All too often a seller has an inflated sense of their home's value because a neighbor sold theirs for a higher price (in a different market)! A Realtor's fiduciary responsibility is to get the best price in the shortest period of time, in the most ethical and professional manner."

—Roberta Alford, Coldwell Banker Gundaker,
St. Louis, Missouri

Chapter 7

Making the Offer: Negotiating the Contract and Price

"I love this house," said Ellie, as she wandered from the kitchen to the living room and the master bedroom, soaking it all in. She and her husband, Richard, wandered the spacious backyard envisioning their puppies running. After three long months of searching, in less than 10 minutes of walking through this home, they knew this was the one.

They wanted it.

"Lets make an offer on this house," said Ellie. Her husband nodded in agreement.

The agent knew the house was getting multiple offers. The goal was to make their offer better than the others. They knew the price was in line with going prices in the area, they had saved up for a tidy earnest money deposit, flexible move-in/closing date (landing it smartly in the seller's hands as a perk), and they offered a fair price they hoped the seller couldn't refuse.

They waited. They are now the proud owners of a four-bedroom rancher. (Their dogs love the backyard.)

When it comes to making an offer, while the price is the most important part, it also includes other important details. The contract will include your financing, down payment, closing costs, inspections you will have, timetables, terms of cancellation, personal property you would like included in the sale (for example, asking for the dishwasher and stove), any needed repairs, closing date, and when you get possession of the property and how to deal with disputes, if any come up. What you genuinely need is a Realtor with good negotiation skills who will not only guide you through this process, but put you in the best position possible.

Hot Tip:

What tactics make you a strong buyer? "Strongest tools for getting the house of your dreams when you find it:

1. Have your financial house in order! (Be pre-approved—not just pre-qualified, for a loan that indicates the top dollar you can afford.)
2. Have no contingencies (must sell house, need to get financing in place). The cleanest contract possible will be the most attractive to a seller.
3. Be reasonable when it comes to any repairs after the inspection."

—Roberta Alford, Coldwell Banker, St. Louis, Missouri

How to Make an Offer

When you find your dream home and you want to make an offer on it, Realtor Ron Roth, principal at Premier Realty gives us these tips for negotiating:

- First, know that the first step in putting yourself in the proper negotiating position is to hire an agent to best represent your interests. Know what is important to you and what is important to the seller.
- Be prepared when writing your offer! Have all of your financing figured out and be pre-approved. You can be the highest priced offer, but if the seller has no idea how you are getting the money, you will instantly be put in a weaker position.
- Know what the market is bearing.

  Seller's market (more buyers than sellers): You probably won't get the property for much less than asking (if not more than asking). Your competition will come from other buyers, so negotiate accordingly. You may have to raise your level of competitiveness in order to make yourself the most attractive buyer in the eyes of the seller.

Buyer's market: You competition is the seller. Find out what is important to the seller, price or terms. If price is more important to you, and terms are more important to the seller, then offer attractive terms and be firm on price. If vice versa, do the opposite. Terms for the seller may be that he/she may have to sell very quickly or just the opposite. He/she may be building a house and may need to stay on the property for an extra three or four months. The seller may be wary of 100 percent financing and therefore may be willing to accept a lower price with more money down.

⇨ The offer "presentation" has an effect as well. Does it include a pre-approval letter, your credit scores, proof of funds, a copy of the deposit check, or a letter from the buyer to the seller? How does the offer look aesthetically? Is it poorly written, is it neatly typed? It is computer generated?

Insiders Insight

"First of all, I write the best offer on behalf of my buyer. The offer not only just includes the cash price, it includes enough time for inspections on the property and any other inspections conducted within the law for the buyer's lender to approve them. And, make sure that if there are any issues—that it is taken care of during a time period called, due diligence—the issues are dealt with or the buyer has the right to cancel the contract."

—Larry Wallenstein, Re/Max Consultants Realty, Fort Lauderdale, Florida.

"All of these things have a profound impression on the seller and their agent. They would much rather work with a buyer (and their agent) if the offer is neat and professional because, it may be a good indication of how the sale will proceed," says Ron. "A sloppy offer and presentation is a good indication that things may go drastically wrong when trying to close."

Accepted, Rejected, or Counteroffered?

Once you submit your offer, it's pretty basic. The seller will either accept your offer, reject it, or counteroffer. Counteroffers tend to deal with price, move-in date, and setting up inspections sooner. Sometimes, if you want to buy the home based on selling yours, sellers will request what's called a kick-out clause. A kick-out clause allows a seller to consider other offers if you aren't able to sell within a certain time frame. Another option sellers use to protect themselves in such instances is a first right of refusal, which is as it sounds: It lets the seller's home stay on the market and if they get a better offer, they can ask you if you want to go through with the purchase or they can accept the more appealing offer. Get all counteroffers and contingencies to the contract in writing. When you and the seller reach an agreement, initial all changes, as well as date and sign final documents—you have a legally binding contract.

Money Savers:

Setting a Great Closing Date:

Faye Brock typically closes on the 20th—25th of the month. If you close toward the end of the month, you won't have a mortgage payment due right a way. For example, her clients that closed around the 20th–25th of October, wouldn't have a mortgage payment due until December 1st (giving them one free month).

—Faye Brock, broker/owner of Century 21
Brock and Associates,
Wilmington, North Carolina

How Much Should Your Earnest Money Be?

Keep in mind, serious offers tend to come with an earnest money deposit (or good faith money) from you. The deposit is five to 10 percent of the sales price and usually goes toward the down payment, but it may be $500 to $1,000, more or less, depending on your ability and on the sales price of the property. You can also do contracts with no earnest money deposits. Earnest money is meant to be enough of a loss to the buyer and fair to the seller if the buyer walks away from the deal. (In most cases, the buyer does get the earnest money back unless it says otherwise in the contract.) A neutral party holds the earnest money deposit and it is deposited after the acceptance of an offer on the contract.

Common Contingencies

A contingency could be described as: "I will buy the house unless..." It's like a big BUT in the middle of a sentence. You can make the purchase of the home contingent on an inspection, appraisal, or getting financing to buy the house. For example, you have the inspection one to two weeks after the signed contract. You find out there are some repairs that need to be taken care of. You may counteroffer again to try lower the price, request repairs, or walk away from the sale.

- Ellie and Richard's contract was contingent on getting a whole house inspection, (a common contingency). They found out the home needed a few minor repairs and they negotiated with the seller to get it fixed before closing. It was a smooth negotiation and they closed on the house a few weeks later.
- Alex also made the purchase of his home contingent on a home inspection. The inspection revealed damage to the garage door, broken hot water heater, leaking pipes, broken storm door, and plumbing issues. The estimated total cost of repairs was more than $3,500. Alex asked for

repairs. The seller refused, saying he was selling his house "as-is." Alex then asked if the seller could credit the cost of repairs at closing. Again, the seller refused, stating the same answer. Unable to come to a compromise, the deal fell apart.

A contingency is really meant to protect your interests in the transaction. That also goes for the ability to get a loan to be able to pay for the home. You will have a period to receive written approval for a loan. (If the deal falls apart, you are usually entitled to your earnest money deposit back.) The Attorney's Title Insurance Fund shares other common contingencies in real estate contracts and what they mean (as seen in *The For Sale By Owner Handbook*):

- Financing Contingency: The deal depends on the buyer being approved for a loan. A buyer will usually specify cancellation rights and return the deposit if they cannot get acceptable financing to purchase the home.
- Inspections: The buyer has a right to a home inspection as well as other inspections specified in the contract. This clause can request the seller to make repairs, lower the price, or the buyer can shake hands with you and walk away from the deal. For more on inspections, visit Chapter 9.
- Clear title: A clear and marketable title to the house.
- Home-sale contingency: The buyer has a specific time frame to sell their current home. Sellers can do a kick-out clause (as mentioned previously). Sometime's sellers would opt to stay on the market and give you a "right of first refusal." For example, if another buyer makes an offer on the seller's home, they would give you two options:

1. Drop the contingency and buy the home.
2. Void the contract. Sometimes buyers ask sellers to take the home off the market for a certain amount of time. Read contingencies carefully—if there is anything you don't understand, ask.

Seller Concessions

What if you need help with closing costs? Be up front with the seller and let them know. Sometimes, you can get a seller to contribute to closing costs. Depending on down payment and programs, it varies how much a seller can contribute toward closing costs. But, Teesie says a good rule of thumb on a conventional loan is:

⇨ If the buyer gives five percent for a down payment, the seller can contribute up to three percent in closing costs.

MONEY SAVER:

Faye Brock recommends the following money-saver tips when buying a home:

- Get a home warranty. All you pay is the service fee and the repairs are made. Get the seller to pay for a home warranty when you buy your home.
- Home inspection. Get a home inspection so you know what you are getting. Negotiate repairs. Also ask the inspector if he does HVAC. (Because if you have to get another person to check that separately, that will come out of your pocket.)
- Home insurance. Know what your home insurance payments are going to be.
- Title insurance. If the seller has the existing title insurance, take the information to the closing coordinator. Don't get new title insurance—tack it onto the existing title insurance (save an additional $300 to $4000).
- Is there a homeowners association in the neighborhood? Read the documents. Do you have a boat? Does the homeowners association not allow for boats to be parked on the property? Are they in a lawsuit and will the member's fees increase? See a copy of the last minutes. (For example, say the association needs money and the association fees are currently $35, but will be $80 next year.)

⇨ If the buyer gives 10 percent on a down payment, the seller could contribute up to 6 percent in closing costs. Teesie says, "It's a rule of thumb, but it changes from product to product." (For more help with closing costs, visit Chapter 8.)

Hot Tip:

"With a condo it is always good to find out how much money the home owners association has in reserves. This will help you understand the likelihood of an assessment. The less they have in reserves the more likely an assessment is."

—Clinton Wade, Estate Agent, President's Circle, Prudential Califirnia Realty, Pacific Design Center, West Hollywood, California

Disclosure/Disclaimer

According to the Attorney's Title Insurance Fund, sample defects the seller should tell you about include damage to the property due to fire, sink holes, floods, problems with major systems in the house (foundations, HVAC, siding, plumbing, and so on.), and sproblems with critters and termites. Sellers should also let you know if the property has any additions made without building permits, environmental hazards (lead based paint for houses built before 1978), and contaminated water/soil. Owners of condos and properties in subdivisions have to give the buyer covenants, conditions, restrictions, and fees/bylaws established by the homeowners association.

If your state requires disclosure, you will receive disclosure paperwork from the seller. (Some states also allow verbal disclosures.) In addition, some federal and local laws require disclosures. According to federal law, if the home is built before 1978, the seller has to disclose known lead-based paint hazards. Check your local, state and federal laws regarding disclosure in your area.

Q & A: Must-Have Negotiation Tactics

If you have a good Realtor, the negotiation process will run smoothly (or it should). Clearly, tell your Realtor what you want to get out of the deal. There will always be some compromises but, honestly, it never hurts to ask for what you want and always address your concerns. For good

pointers during the contract-negotiation process, contingencies to protect you during the deal, how to walk away from the deal, as well as what to do when an offer is accepted, countered or rejected, we asked Tara Nicholle Nelson, Esq. She shared insight from her book, *The Savvy Woman's Homebuying Handbook.*

Piper: What are good pointers during the contract-negotiation process?

Tara:

1. It Takes Two—Even after you get into contract, EVERY document needs to be signed by both you and the seller. Every counter, every addendum, every disclosure, every EVERYTHING gets signed by everyone.
2. The "No Handshake" Rule: There's no such thing as a "verbal" agreement when it comes to real estate. No matter how small the item being discussed—a couple of extra days to close escrow, the seller's agreement to replace a window, whatever—get it in writing or don't count on it!
3. Be Quick on the Uptake: It is critical to respond to counteroffers as soon as possible, and to avoid making a counteroffer as to any term that is not truly a deal breaker. Delays in responding leave space open for another buyer to step in and create a bidding war, or even more likely, for the seller to perceive that other, serious buyers might be out there—a seller's mere perception of a hint of a whiff of the scent of a potential bidding war is a homebuyer's number one nemesis, ratcheting up the possible sales price in the seller's head on an exponential basis.
4. Cutting in the Middle(wo)man: When you want to ask or tell the seller something, always, always, always go through your Realtor, who will communicate your request or concern to the seller's agent. I know it seems inefficient, but it is truly a rookie move to contact the seller directly—it's just

not done, mostly because the terminology is tough to master and legally sensitive. Also, some seemingly innocent and minor changes to your agreement with the seller might create problems with your lender; your Realtor is better equipped than you to see these red flags. You hired your agent, so use her! It will prevent the catastrophic misunderstandings (read: drama) that can result when you or the seller says something even slightly different than what you each actually mean!

Piper: What contingencies should you have in your contract to protect your interests?

Tara: My fancy definition for a contingency is the buyer's "right to bail" out of the contract for a particular reason, without losing their earnest money deposit. Note: Some states have option or objection periods, rather than the contingency structure. There are tons of contingencies buyers may put in their contracts; my average client includes contingencies for everything from appraisal (the buyer can bail without penalty if the property doesn't appraise at the purchase price), to insurability (the buyer can bail if they can't find insurance for the property). If a buyer is purchasing a property for a specific purpose or with specific intentions, they should consider instituting a contingency giving them the right to back out of the deal if the property turns out to be unsuitable for their particular purpose.

Often, though, writing a "clean" or competitive offer means minimizing the number of contingencies in your offer. The two contingencies buyers should insist on having in their contracts are the *loan* and *inspection* contingencies. The loan contingency allows you to be certain that your lender's underwriter will approve of all your documentation and your property (including its HOA, if applicable), and make a final commitment to fund the loan. The only hypothetical situation which eliminates the need for a loan contingency is one where you are paying cash for the property.

The inspection contingency is the one that allows you to back out of the deal if you are not satisfied with the results of your investigations into the condition and insurability of the property. Unless you are ready, willing, and able to buy the property at the price and terms of the original property no matter what condition it is in (for example, a brand new home with comprehensive builder's and home warranties, or a home you knew was a teardown at the outset), you need this contingency for at least as many days as it will take you to have the necessary inspections, and read and review the inspectors' reports.

Piper: When can you or the seller walk away from the deal?

Tara: In many states, the seller's hands are pretty much tied (legally speaking) once you are in contract, unless and until you (the buyer) breach the contract in a material way. If you fail to provide a loan commitment letter, your deposit check never comes in or bounces, you fail to remove your contingencies when you agreed to (and after a notice from the seller that you'd better remove them or the deal is kaput), or you fail to actually come up with the funding to close the deal, the seller can walk away.

You have much more leeway as the buyer. You can back out at any time until closing, technically, but will be on the hook for your deposit money (at the very least) if you back out after your contingency, option or objection period has run, according to the terms of your contract. If you are in a contingency contract, you are most likely required to actually proactively exercise (bail) or remove (agree to move forward) your contingencies by signing and submitting a form, and you can back out of the contract until you have done that without losing more than the money you've paid the inspectors. If you are in an option contract (used in many southwestern states, such as New Mexico and Texas), you can only back out penalty-free until your option period expires, unless you extend it in writing signed by the seller. In those states, you lose only your option fee (almost never more than $100) if you back out before the end of your option period.

Piper: What to do if your offer is accepted, rejected, or counteroffered?

Tara: Once your offer is accepted, your Realtor will open escrow and your contingency or option period clock will start ticking, so you'll have a couple of weeks filled with inspections and reviewing disclosures and reports.

If your offer is rejected outright, which is very rare, the seller is flat out telling you that, either, they would rather not sell to you than to try to counter your offer. You can infer from this that either they have sold the house to someone else or that your offer terms were very far from acceptable to them. If you really want that particular house, have your Realtor call the listing agent to drill deeper into the reasons underlying the seller's response, and consider resubmitting an offer that is significantly closer to the seller's desired terms, per the listing agent. If, however, your original offer was as high in price as you can go (and still afford the house), that just might not be the house for you, and your house hunt should continue.

If the seller makes a counteroffer, then the onus is on you and your Realtor to review the counteroffer and decide whether the terms therein work for you or not. If so, accept it, and move on. If not, you may either reject the offer or issue another counteroffer, altering only the counteroffer terms that were unacceptable to you. You and the seller can go back and forth in counteroffers ad infinitum until you reach a meeting of the minds on all terms, but you should be aware that, until one is accepted, another buyer can always walk in and snag the property out from under you, so try to keep the counters to a minimum. Make sure you're only negotiating on absolute deal-breakers so that you don't lose your dream home over the question of who pays for that $300 home warranty.

Source: *The Savvy Woman's Homebuying Handbook* (Prosperity Way Press) by Tara Nicholle Nelson, Esq.

What Does That Mean?

What are the common legal terms you should know on your contract? We asked Jeffrey P. Zane, P.A., for advice. Following, the president of the Attorneys' Real Estate Council of Palm Beach County, Inc., Florida, shares with us terms and definitions we should know:

Effective Date: The date that the last of the parties to the contract sign the document. It is important because it is from that date that all of the calculations for timely compliance with the contract's terms are calculated. An example of this is that the financing application must be submitted within five (5) days after effective date.

Financing Contingency: The inclusion of this clause makes the contract contingent upon the buyer(s) obtaining approval of a loan. It requires the buyer(s) to use reasonable diligence to obtain the loan. It further requires the buyer(s) to timely communicate with the seller(s) the status of its efforts to obtain the loan. Failure to properly communicate with the seller may nullify the buyer(s)'s ability to obtain its deposit back even if the buyer(s) fail to obtain the financing.

Closing Date: This is the date by which the contract calls for the sale and purchase to take place. It is on that date that the money is transferred to the seller(s) and the deed and mortgage, if any, are executed by the seller(s) and the buyer(s) respectively.

Homeowners or Condominium Disclosure: When the buyer(s) is purchasing either a single family home in a Homeowners' Community or a condominium in a Condominium Community the seller(s) must give the buyer(s) a disclosure that reflects the fees, approvals, and/or assessments relating to the association. The buyer(s) is also given three (3) days to review the Association Documents during which time the buyer(s) can get their deposit back and terminate the contract without penalty.

Survey: A licensed surveyor reviews the property to determine if the are any encroachments onto the property by an adjacent property owner's improvements. The surveyor would also determine if the improvements being purchased falls onto the adjacent property. It would also determine if there are any setbacks and/or restriction violations. The buyer(s) are required to obtain a survey if there is a loan involved and should obtain a survey even if it is buying the property for cash.

Deed: This is the document that is recorded in the public records and transfers title of the real estate from the seller(s) to the buyer(s).

Bill of Sale: This is the document that is not recorded in the public records, but it effectively transfers the personal property that is included in the sale of the real estate.

Mortgage: This is the document that is recorded in the public records and creates a lien on the real estate to secure the real estate as collateral for the loan.

Prorations: There are periodic payments in real estate such as real estate taxes. That payment covers a time frame of January 1st through December 31st. The cost of that real estate tax is prorated to reflect the portion of the year that the seller(s) are required to pay and a portion of the year that the Buyer(s) are required to pay. The same calculation would be required if there were association assessments, or rental income, and so on.

Seller Disclosure: This requires the seller(s) to inform the buyer(s) of any fact(s) that the seller(s) knows of that materially affects the value of the property which are not readily observable by the buyer(s).

1031 Exchange: This refers to a tax-free exchange that may be available to either seller(s) or buyer(s) that are involved in an investment or commercial real estate transaction.

Windstorm Insurance: This involves insurance protecting against damage caused by wind typically in conjunction with a hurricane or tornado.

Flood Insurance: This involves insurance protecting against damage caused by water flowing from the ground up and not from the sky down.

Homeowner's Insurance: This involves insurance protecting against damages caused by fire, theft, or negligence involving persons on the property, and so on.

Balance to Close Requirements: As part of the real estate closing the closing agent will inform the parties the amount of money they need to bring to the closing in order to complete the transaction. These moneys need to be delivered to the closing agent no later than the time of the closing. The moneys must either be in the form of a wire transfer received by the closing agent or a *locally drawn* cashier's or official bank check.

CALIFORNIA ASSOCIATION OF REALTORS®

CALIFORNIA
RESIDENTIAL PURCHASE AGREEMENT
AND JOINT ESCROW INSTRUCTIONS
For Use With Single Family Residential Property — Attached or Detached
(C.A.R. Form RPA-CA, Revised 1/06)

Date *June 19, 2007*, at *Oakland*, California.

1. **OFFER:**
   A. **THIS IS AN OFFER FROM** *Jonathan A. Buyer, Jacqueline A. Buyer* ("Buyer").
   B. **THE REAL PROPERTY TO BE ACQUIRED** is described as *560 La Mirada Drive, Oakland CA 94619* , Assessor's Parcel No. *999999999999* , situated in *Oakland* , County of *Alameda* , California, ("Property").
   C. **THE PURCHASE PRICE** offered is *Five Hundred Fifty Thousand* Dollars $ *550,000.00* .
   D. **CLOSE OF ESCROW** shall occur on *July 19, 2007* (date) (or ☐ ______ **Days** After Acceptance).
2. **FINANCE TERMS:** Obtaining the loans below **is a contingency** of this Agreement unless: (i) either 2K or 2L is checked below; or (ii) otherwise agreed in writing. Buyer shall act diligently and in good faith to obtain the designated loans. Obtaining deposit, down payment and closing costs **is not a contingency.** Buyer represents that funds will be good when deposited with Escrow Holder.
   A. **INITIAL DEPOSIT:** Buyer has given a deposit in the amount of . . . . $ *5,500.00*
   to the agent submitting the offer (or to ☐ ______), by personal check (or ☐ ______), made payable to *ABC Title Company* , which shall be held uncashed until Acceptance and then deposited within 3 business days after Acceptance (or ☐ ______), with Escrow Holder, (or ☐ into Broker's trust account).
   B. **INCREASED DEPOSIT:** Buyer shall deposit with Escrow Holder an increased deposit in the amount of . . . . $ *11,000.00*
   within ______ **Days** After Acceptance, or ☒ *upon removal of all contingencies*
   C. **FIRST LOAN IN THE AMOUNT OF** . . . . $ *440,000.00*
   (1) NEW First Deed of Trust in favor of lender, encumbering the Property, securing a note payable at maximum interest of *7.000* % fixed rate, or *6.750* % initial adjustable rate with a maximum interest rate of *10.000* %, balance due in *30* years, amortized over *25* years. Buyer shall pay loan fees/points not to exceed *2* . (These terms apply whether the designated loan is conventional, FHA or VA.)
   (2) ☐ FHA ☐ VA: (The following terms only apply to the FHA or VA loan that is checked.) Seller shall pay ______ % discount points. Seller shall pay other fees not allowed to be paid by Buyer, ☐ not to exceed $ ______ . Seller shall pay the cost of lender required Repairs (including those for wood destroying pest) not otherwise provided for in this Agreement, ☐ not to exceed $ ______ . (Actual loan amount may increase if mortgage insurance premiums, funding fees or closing costs are financed.)
   D. **ADDITIONAL FINANCING TERMS:** ☐ Seller financing, (C.A.R. Form SFA); ☒ secondary financing, ... $ *55,000.00*
   (C.A.R. Form PAA, paragraph 4A); ☐ assumed financing (C.A.R. Form PAA, paragraph 4B)
   E. **BALANCE OF PURCHASE PRICE** (not including costs of obtaining loans and other closing costs) in the amount of . . $ *38,500.00*
   to be deposited with Escrow Holder within sufficient time to close escrow.
   F. **PURCHASE PRICE (TOTAL):** . . . . $ *550,000.00*
   G. **LOAN APPLICATIONS:** Within 7 (or ☒ *prior to*) **Days** After Acceptance, Buyer shall provide Seller a letter from lender or mortgage loan broker stating that, based on a review of Buyer's written application and credit report, Buyer is prequalified or preapproved for the NEW loan specified in 2C above.
   H. **VERIFICATION OF DOWN PAYMENT AND CLOSING COSTS:** Buyer (or Buyer's lender or loan broker pursuant to 2G) shall, within 7 (or ☐ ______) **Days** After Acceptance, provide Seller written verification of Buyer's down payment and closing costs.
   I. **LOAN CONTINGENCY REMOVAL:** (i) Within 17 (or ☐ ______) **Days** After Acceptance, Buyer shall, as specified in paragraph 14, remove the loan contingency or cancel this Agreement; **OR** (ii) (if checked) ☐ the loan contingency shall remain in effect until the designated loans are funded.
   J. **APPRAISAL CONTINGENCY AND REMOVAL:** This Agreement is (**OR**, if checked, ☐ is NOT) contingent upon the Property appraising at no less than the specified purchase price. If there is a loan contingency, at the time the loan contingency is removed (or, if checked, ☐ within 17 (or ______) Days After Acceptance), Buyer shall, as specified in paragraph 14B(3), remove the appraisal contingency or cancel this Agreement. If there is no loan contingency, Buyer shall, as specified in paragraph 14B(3), remove the appraisal contingency within 17 (or ______) Days After Acceptance.
   K. ☐ **NO LOAN CONTINGENCY** (If checked): Obtaining any loan in paragraphs 2C, 2D or elsewhere in this Agreement is NOT a contingency of this Agreement. If Buyer does not obtain the loan and as a result Buyer does not purchase the Property, Seller may be entitled to Buyer's deposit or other legal remedies.
   L. ☐ **ALL CASH OFFER** (If checked): No loan is needed to purchase the Property. Buyer shall, within 7 (or ☐ ______) **Days** After Acceptance, provide Seller written verification of sufficient funds to close this transaction.
3. **CLOSING AND OCCUPANCY:**
   A. Buyer intends (or ☐ does not intend) to occupy the Property as Buyer's primary residence.
   B. **Seller-occupied or vacant property:** Occupancy shall be delivered to Buyer at *1:00* ☐ AM ☒ PM, ☒ on the date of Close Of Escrow; ☐ on ______ ; or ☐ no later than ______ **Days** After Close Of Escrow. (C.A.R. Form PAA, paragraph 2.) If transfer of title and occupancy do not occur at the same time, Buyer and Seller are advised to: (i) enter into a written occupancy agreement; and (ii) consult with their insurance and legal advisors.

Buyer's Initials (______) (______)
Seller's Initials (______) (______)
Reviewed by ______ Date ______

EQUAL HOUSING OPPORTUNITY

Agent: Tara-Nicholle Nelson Phone: (510) 910 - 6713 Fax: (510) 291 - 9715 Prepared using WINForms® software
Broker: Tara-Nicholle Nelson, Broker 560 Vernon Street Oakland, CA 94610

Property Address: *560 La Mirada Drive Oakland, CA 94619* Date: *June 19, 2007*

C. **Tenant-occupied property: (i) Property shall be vacant** at least **5 (or ☐ ______) Days** Prior to Close Of Escrow, unless otherwise agreed in writing. **Note to Seller: If you are unable to deliver Property vacant in accordance with rent control and other applicable Law, you may be in breach of this Agreement.**

OR (ii) (if checked) ☐ **Tenant to remain in possession.** The attached addendum is incorporated into this Agreement (C.A.R. Form PAA, paragraph 3.);

OR (iii) (if checked) ☐ **This Agreement is contingent** upon Buyer and Seller entering into a written agreement regarding occupancy of the Property within the time specified in paragraph 14B(1). If no written agreement is reached within this time, either Buyer or Seller may cancel this Agreement in writing.

D. At Close Of Escrow, Seller assigns to Buyer any assignable warranty rights for items included in the sale and shall provide any available Copies of such warranties. Brokers cannot and will not determine the assignability of any warranties.

E. At Close Of Escrow, unless otherwise agreed in writing, Seller shall provide keys and/or means to operate all locks, mailboxes, security systems, alarms and garage door openers. If Property is a condominium or located in a common interest subdivision, Buyer may be required to pay a deposit to the Homeowners' Association ("HOA") to obtain keys to accessible HOA facilities.

4. **ALLOCATION OF COSTS** (If checked): Unless otherwise specified here, this paragraph only determines who is to pay for the report, inspection, test or service mentioned. If not specified here or elsewhere in this Agreement, the determination of who is to pay for any work recommended or identified by any such report, inspection, test or service shall be by the method specified in paragraph 14B(2).

A. **WOOD DESTROYING PEST INSPECTION:**

(1) ☒ Buyer ☐ Seller shall pay for an inspection and report for wood destroying pests and organisms ("Report") which shall be prepared by *ACE Termite Company*, a registered structural pest control company. The Report shall cover the accessible areas of the main building and attached structures and, if checked: ☒ detached garages and carports, ☒ detached decks, ☒ the following other structures or areas *fences* ______. The Report shall not include roof coverings. If Property is a condominium or located in a common interest subdivision, the Report shall include only the separate interest and any exclusive-use areas being transferred and shall not include common areas, unless otherwise agreed. Water tests of shower pans on upper level units may not be performed without consent of the owners of property below the shower.

OR (2) ☐ **(If checked)** The attached addendum (C.A.R. Form WPA) regarding wood destroying pest inspection and allocation of cost is incorporated into this Agreement.

B. **OTHER INSPECTIONS AND REPORTS:**

(1) ☐ Buyer ☒ Seller shall pay to have septic or private sewage disposal systems inspected ______.

(2) ☐ Buyer ☐ Seller shall pay to have domestic wells tested for water potability and productivity *N/A*.

(3) ☐ Buyer ☒ Seller shall pay for a natural hazard zone disclosure report prepared by *XYZ Geologists*.

(4) ☐ Buyer ☒ Seller shall pay for the following inspection or report *Megan's Law, Tax Database, EnviroCheck*.

(5) ☒ Buyer ☐ Seller shall pay for the following inspection or report *Property, Roof & Any Buyer Deems Nec.*

C. **GOVERNMENT REQUIREMENTS AND RETROFIT:**

(1) ☐ Buyer ☒ Seller shall pay for smoke detector installation and/or water heater bracing, if required by Law. Prior to Close Of Escrow, Seller shall provide Buyer a written statement of compliance in accordance with state and local Law, unless exempt.

(2) ☐ Buyer ☒ Seller shall pay the cost of compliance with any other minimum mandatory government retrofit standards, inspections and reports if required as a condition of closing escrow under any Law ______.

D. **ESCROW AND TITLE:**

(1) ☒ Buyer ☐ Seller shall pay escrow fee ______.
Escrow Holder shall be *ABC Title Company*.

(2) ☒ Buyer ☐ Seller shall pay for **owner's** title insurance policy specified in paragraph 12E ______.
Owner's title policy to be issued by *ABC Title Company*.
(Buyer shall pay for any title insurance policy insuring Buyer's **lender**, unless otherwise agreed in writing.)

E. **OTHER COSTS:**

(1) ☐ Buyer ☒ Seller shall pay County transfer tax or transfer fee ______.

(2) ☒ Buyer ☒ Seller shall pay City transfer tax or transfer fee *50/50 split*.

(3) ☐ Buyer ☐ Seller shall pay HOA transfer fee *N/A*.

(4) ☐ Buyer ☐ Seller shall pay HOA document preparation fees *N/A*.

(5) ☐ Buyer ☒ Seller shall pay the cost, not to exceed $ *350.00*, of a one-year home warranty plan, issued by *LMNOP Home Protection Plans*, with the following optional coverage: *First Class Upgrade*.

(6) ☐ Buyer ☒ Seller shall pay for *professional cleaning of property after seller moves out*.

(7) ☐ Buyer ☐ Seller shall pay for ______.

5. **STATUTORY DISCLOSURES (INCLUDING LEAD-BASED PAINT HAZARD DISCLOSURES) AND CANCELLATION RIGHTS:**

A. (1) Seller shall, within the time specified in paragraph 14A, deliver to Buyer, if required by Law: **(i)** Federal Lead-Based Paint Disclosures and pamphlet ("Lead Disclosures"); and **(ii)** disclosures or notices required by sections 1102 et. seq. and 1103 et. seq. of the California Civil Code ("Statutory Disclosures"). Statutory Disclosures include, but are not limited to, a Real Estate Transfer Disclosure Statement ("TDS"), Natural Hazard Disclosure Statement ("NHD"), notice or actual knowledge of release of illegal controlled substance, notice of special tax and/or assessments (or, if allowed, substantially equivalent notice regarding the Mello-Roos Community Facilities Act and Improvement Bond Act of 1915) and, if Seller has actual knowledge, an industrial use and military ordnance location disclosure (C.A.R. Form SSD).

(2) Buyer shall, within the time specified in paragraph 14B(1), return Signed Copies of the Statutory and Lead Disclosures to Seller.

(3) In the event Seller, prior to Close Of Escrow, becomes aware of adverse conditions materially affecting the Property, or any material inaccuracy in disclosures, information or representations previously provided to Buyer of which Buyer is otherwise unaware, Seller shall promptly provide a subsequent or amended disclosure or notice, in writing, covering those items. **However, a subsequent or amended disclosure shall not be required for conditions and material inaccuracies disclosed in reports ordered and paid for by Buyer.**

Buyer's Initials (______) (______)
Seller's Initials (______) (______)

Reviewed by ______ Date ______

Jonathan and J

Property Address: *560 La Mirada Drive Oakland, CA 94619* Date: *June 19, 2007*

(4) If any disclosure or notice specified in 5A(1), or subsequent or amended disclosure or notice is delivered to Buyer after the offer is Signed, Buyer shall have the right to cancel this Agreement within **3 Days** After delivery in person, or **5 Days** After delivery by deposit in the mail, by giving written notice of cancellation to Seller or Seller's agent. (Lead Disclosures sent by mail must be sent certified mail or better.)

(5) **Note to Buyer and Seller: Waiver of Statutory and Lead Disclosures is prohibited by Law.**

B. **NATURAL AND ENVIRONMENTAL HAZARDS:** Within the time specified in paragraph 14A, Seller shall, if required by Law: **(i)** deliver to Buyer earthquake guides (and questionnaire) and environmental hazards booklet; **(ii)** even if exempt from the obligation to provide a NHD, disclose if the Property is located in a Special Flood Hazard Area; Potential Flooding (Inundation) Area; Very High Fire Hazard Zone; State Fire Responsibility Area; Earthquake Fault Zone; Seismic Hazard Zone; and **(iii)** disclose any other zone as required by Law and provide any other information required for those zones.

C. **DATA BASE DISCLOSURE:** Notice: Pursuant to Section 290.46 of the Penal Code, information about specified registered sex offenders is made available to the public via an Internet Web site maintained by the Department of Justice at www.meganslaw.ca.gov. Depending on an offender's criminal history, this information will include either the address at which the offender resides or the community of residence and ZIP Code in which he or she resides. (Neither Seller nor Brokers are required to check this website. If Buyer wants further information, Broker recommends that Buyer obtain information from this website during Buyer's inspection contingency period. Brokers do not have expertise in this area.)

6. **CONDOMINIUM/PLANNED UNIT DEVELOPMENT DISCLOSURES:**

A. **SELLER HAS: 7 (or ☐ ____________) Days** After Acceptance to disclose to Buyer whether the Property is a condominium, or is located in a planned unit development or other common interest subdivision (C.A.R. Form SSD).

B. If the Property is a condominium or is located in a planned unit development or other common interest subdivision, Seller has **3** (or ☐ ________) **Days** After Acceptance to request from the HOA (C.A.R. Form HOA): **(i)** Copies of any documents required by Law; **(ii)** disclosure of any pending or anticipated claim or litigation by or against the HOA; **(iii)** a statement containing the location and number of designated parking and storage spaces; **(iv)** Copies of the most recent 12 months of HOA minutes for regular and special meetings; and **(v)** the names and contact information of all HOAs governing the Property (collectively, "CI Disclosures"). Seller shall itemize and deliver to Buyer all CI Disclosures received from the HOA and any CI Disclosures in Seller's possession. Buyer's approval of CI Disclosures is a contingency of this Agreement as specified in paragraph 14B(3).

7. **CONDITIONS AFFECTING PROPERTY:**

A. Unless otherwise agreed: **(i) the Property is sold (a) in its PRESENT physical condition as of the date of Acceptance and (b) subject to Buyer's Investigation rights; (ii)** the Property, including pool, spa, landscaping and grounds, is to be maintained in substantially the same condition as on the date of Acceptance; and **(iii)** all debris and personal property not included in the sale shall be removed by Close Of Escrow.

B. **SELLER SHALL, within the time specified in paragraph 14A, DISCLOSE KNOWN MATERIAL FACTS AND DEFECTS affecting the Property, including known insurance claims within the past five years, AND MAKE OTHER DISCLOSURES REQUIRED BY LAW (C.A.R. Form SSD).**

C. **NOTE TO BUYER: You are strongly advised to conduct investigations of the entire Property in order to determine its present condition since Seller may not be aware of all defects affecting the Property or other factors that you consider important. Property improvements may not be built according to code, in compliance with current Law, or have had permits issued.**

D. **NOTE TO SELLER: Buyer has the right to inspect the Property and, as specified in paragraph 14B, based upon information discovered in those inspections: (i) cancel this Agreement; or (ii) request that you make Repairs or take other action.**

8. **ITEMS INCLUDED AND EXCLUDED:**

A. **NOTE TO BUYER AND SELLER:** Items listed as included or excluded in the MLS, flyers or marketing materials are **not** included in the purchase price or excluded from the sale unless specified in 8B or C.

B. **ITEMS INCLUDED IN SALE:**

(1) All EXISTING fixtures and fittings that are attached to the Property;

(2) Existing electrical, mechanical, lighting, plumbing and heating fixtures, ceiling fans, fireplace inserts, gas logs and grates, solar systems, built-in appliances, window and door screens, awnings, shutters, window coverings, attached floor coverings, television antennas, satellite dishes, private integrated telephone systems, air coolers/conditioners, pool/spa equipment, garage door openers/remote controls, mailbox, in-ground landscaping, trees/shrubs, water softeners, water purifiers, security systems/alarms; and

(3) The following items: *all pottery in back yard garden, washer, dryer and refrigerator*

(4) Seller represents that all items included in the purchase price, unless otherwise specified, are owned by Seller.

(5) All items included shall be transferred free of liens and without Seller warranty.

C. **ITEMS EXCLUDED FROM SALE:** *oil cans in garage, aluminum storage shed in back yard*

9. **BUYER'S INVESTIGATION OF PROPERTY AND MATTERS AFFECTING PROPERTY:**

A. Buyer's acceptance of the condition of, and any other matter affecting the Property, is a contingency of this Agreement as specified in this paragraph and paragraph 14B. Within the time specified in paragraph 14B(1), Buyer shall have the right, at Buyer's expense unless otherwise agreed, to conduct inspections, investigations, tests, surveys and other studies ("Buyer Investigations"), including, but not limited to, the right to: **(i)** inspect for lead-based paint and other lead-based paint hazards; **(ii)** inspect for wood destroying pests and organisms; **(iii)** review the registered sex offender database; **(iv)** confirm the insurability of Buyer and the Property; and **(v)** satisfy Buyer as to any matter specified in the attached Buyer's Inspection Advisory (C.A.R. Form BIA). Without Seller's prior written consent, Buyer shall neither make nor cause to be made: **(i)** invasive or destructive Buyer Investigations; or **(ii)** inspections by any governmental building or zoning inspector or government employee, unless required by Law.

B. Buyer shall complete Buyer Investigations and, as specified in paragraph 14B, remove the contingency or cancel this Agreement. Buyer shall give Seller, at no cost, complete Copies of all Buyer Investigation reports obtained by Buyer. Seller shall make the Property available for all Buyer Investigations. Seller shall have water, gas, electricity and all operable pilot lights on for Buyer's Investigations and through the date possession is made available to Buyer.

Buyer's Initials (________)(________)
Seller's Initials (________)(________)

Reviewed by __________ Date __________

Property Address: *560 La Mirada Drive Oakland, CA 94619* Date: *June 19, 2007*

10. REPAIRS: Repairs shall be completed prior to final verification of condition unless otherwise agreed in writing. Repairs to be performed at Seller's expense may be performed by Seller or through others, provided that the work complies with applicable Law, including governmental permit, inspection and approval requirements. Repairs shall be performed in a good, skillful manner with materials of quality and appearance comparable to existing materials. It is understood that exact restoration of appearance or cosmetic items following all Repairs may not be possible. Seller shall: (i) obtain receipts for Repairs performed by others; (ii) prepare a written statement indicating the Repairs performed by Seller and the date of such Repairs; and (iii) provide Copies of receipts and statements to Buyer prior to final verification of condition.

11. BUYER INDEMNITY AND SELLER PROTECTION FOR ENTRY UPON PROPERTY: Buyer shall: (i) keep the Property free and clear of liens; (ii) Repair all damage arising from Buyer Investigations; and (iii) indemnify and hold Seller harmless from all resulting liability, claims, demands, damages and costs. Buyer shall carry, or Buyer shall require anyone acting on Buyer's behalf to carry, policies of liability, workers' compensation and other applicable insurance, defending and protecting Seller from liability for any injuries to persons or property occurring during any Buyer Investigations or work done on the Property at Buyer's direction prior to Close Of Escrow. Seller is advised that certain protections may be afforded Seller by recording a "Notice of Non-responsibility" (C.A.R. Form NNR) for Buyer Investigations and work done on the Property at Buyer's direction. Buyer's obligations under this paragraph shall survive the termination of this Agreement.

12. TITLE AND VESTING:

A. Within the time specified in paragraph 14, Buyer shall be provided a current preliminary (title) report, which is only an offer by the title insurer to issue a policy of title insurance and may not contain every item affecting title. Buyer's review of the preliminary report and any other matters which may affect title are a contingency of this Agreement as specified in paragraph 14B.

B. Title is taken in its present condition subject to all encumbrances, easements, covenants, conditions, restrictions, rights and other matters, whether of record or not, as of the date of Acceptance except: (i) monetary liens of record unless Buyer is assuming those obligations or taking the Property subject to those obligations; and (ii) those matters which Seller has agreed to remove in writing.

C. Within the time specified in paragraph 14A, Seller has a duty to disclose to Buyer all matters known to Seller affecting title, whether of record or not.

D. At Close Of Escrow, Buyer shall receive a grant deed conveying title (or, for stock cooperative or long-term lease, an assignment of stock certificate or of Seller's leasehold interest), including oil, mineral and water rights if currently owned by Seller. Title shall vest as designated in Buyer's supplemental escrow instructions. THE MANNER OF TAKING TITLE MAY HAVE SIGNIFICANT LEGAL AND TAX CONSEQUENCES. CONSULT AN APPROPRIATE PROFESSIONAL.

E. Buyer shall receive a CLTA/ALTA Homeowner's Policy of Title Insurance. A title company, at Buyer's request, can provide information about the availability, desirability, coverage, and cost of various title insurance coverages and endorsements. If Buyer desires title coverage other than that required by this paragraph, Buyer shall instruct Escrow Holder in writing and pay any increase in cost.

13. SALE OF BUYER'S PROPERTY:

A. This Agreement is NOT contingent upon the sale of any property owned by Buyer.

OR B. ☐ (If checked): The attached addendum (C.A.R. Form COP) regarding the contingency for the sale of property owned by Buyer is incorporated into this Agreement.

14. TIME PERIODS; REMOVAL OF CONTINGENCIES; CANCELLATION RIGHTS: The following time periods may only be extended, altered, modified or changed by mutual written agreement. Any removal of contingencies or cancellation under this paragraph must be in writing (C.A.R. Form CR).

A. **SELLER HAS: 7 (or ☐ ____________) Days** After Acceptance to deliver to Buyer all reports, disclosures and information for which Seller is responsible under paragraphs 4, 5A and B, 6A, 7B and 12.

B. (1) **BUYER HAS: 17 (or ☐ ____________) Days** After Acceptance, unless otherwise agreed in writing, to:

(i) complete all Buyer Investigations; approve all disclosures, reports and other applicable information, which Buyer receives from Seller; and approve all matters affecting the Property (including lead-based paint and lead-based paint hazards as well as other information specified in paragraph 5 and insurability of Buyer and the Property); and

(ii) return to Seller Signed Copies of Statutory and Lead Disclosures delivered by Seller in accordance with paragraph 5A.

(2) Within the time specified in 14B(1), Buyer may request that Seller make repairs or take any other action regarding the Property (C.A.R. Form RR). Seller has no obligation to agree to or respond to Buyer's requests.

(3) By the end of the time specified in 14B(1) (or 2I for loan contingency or 2J for appraisal contingency), Buyer shall, in writing, remove the applicable contingency (C.A.R. Form CR) or cancel this Agreement. However, if (i) government-mandated inspections/ reports required as a condition of closing; or (ii) Common Interest Disclosures pursuant to paragraph 6B are not made within the time specified in 14A, then Buyer has **5 (or ☐ ______________) Days** After receipt of any such items, or the time specified in 14B(1), whichever is later, to remove the applicable contingency or cancel this Agreement in writing.

C. **CONTINUATION OF CONTINGENCY OR CONTRACTUAL OBLIGATION; SELLER RIGHT TO CANCEL:**

(1) **Seller right to Cancel; Buyer Contingencies:** Seller, after first giving Buyer a Notice to Buyer to Perform (as specified below), may cancel this Agreement in writing and authorize return of Buyer's deposit if, by the time specified in this Agreement, Buyer does not remove in writing the applicable contingency or cancel this Agreement. Once all contingencies have been removed, failure of either Buyer or Seller to close escrow on time may be a breach of this Agreement.

(2) **Continuation of Contingency:** Even after the expiration of the time specified in 14B, Buyer retains the right to make requests to Seller, remove in writing the applicable contingency or cancel this Agreement until Seller cancels pursuant to 14C(1). Once Seller receives Buyer's written removal of all contingencies, Seller may not cancel this Agreement pursuant to 14C(1).

(3) **Seller right to Cancel; Buyer Contract Obligations:** Seller, after first giving Buyer a Notice to Buyer to Perform (as specified below), may cancel this Agreement in writing and authorize return of Buyer's deposit for any of the following reasons: (i) if Buyer fails to deposit funds as required by 2A or 2B; (ii) if the funds deposited pursuant to 2A or 2B are not good when deposited; (iii) if Buyer fails to provide a letter as required by 2G; (iv) if Buyer fails to provide verification as required by 2H or 2L; (v) if Seller reasonably disapproves of the verification provided by 2H or 2L; (vi) if Buyer fails to return Statutory and Lead Disclosures as required by paragraph 5A(2); or (vii) if Buyer fails to sign or initial a separate liquidated damage form for an increased deposit as required by paragraph 16. **Seller is not required to give Buyer a Notice to Perform regarding Close of Escrow.**

(4) **Notice To Buyer To Perform:** The Notice to Buyer to Perform (C.A.R. Form NBP) shall: (i) be in writing; (ii) be signed by Seller; and (iii) give Buyer at least **24** (or ☐ _______) hours (or until the time specified in the applicable paragraph, whichever occurs last) to take the applicable action. A Notice to Buyer to Perform may not be given any earlier than **2 Days** Prior to the expiration of the applicable time for Buyer to remove a contingency or cancel this Agreement or meet a 14C(3) obligation.

Buyer's Initials (________)(________)
Seller's Initials (________)(________)

Reviewed by ________ Date ________

Property Address: 560 La Mirada Drive Oakland, CA 94619 Date: June 19, 2007

D. **EFFECT OF BUYER'S REMOVAL OF CONTINGENCIES:** If Buyer removes, in writing, any contingency or cancellation rights, unless otherwise specified in a separate written agreement between Buyer and Seller, Buyer shall conclusively be deemed to have: (i) completed all Buyer Investigations, and review of reports and other applicable information and disclosures pertaining to that contingency or cancellation right; (ii) elected to proceed with the transaction; and (iii) assumed all liability, responsibility and expense for Repairs or corrections pertaining to that contingency or cancellation right, or for inability to obtain financing.

E. **EFFECT OF CANCELLATION ON DEPOSITS:** If Buyer or Seller gives written notice of cancellation pursuant to rights duly exercised under the terms of this Agreement, Buyer and Seller agree to Sign mutual instructions to cancel the sale and escrow and release deposits to the party entitled to the funds, less fees and costs incurred by that party. Fees and costs may be payable to service providers and vendors for services and products provided during escrow. **Release of funds will require mutual Signed release instructions from Buyer and Seller, judicial decision or arbitration award. A party may be subject to a civil penalty of up to $1,000 for refusal to sign such instructions if no good faith dispute exists as to who is entitled to the deposited funds (Civil Code §1057.3).**

15. **FINAL VERIFICATION OF CONDITION:** Buyer shall have the right to make a final inspection of the Property within 5 (or ____________) **Days** Prior to Close Of Escrow, NOT AS A CONTINGENCY OF THE SALE, but solely to confirm: (i) the Property is maintained pursuant to paragraph 7A; (ii) Repairs have been completed as agreed; and (iii) Seller has complied with Seller's other obligations under this Agreement.

16. **LIQUIDATED DAMAGES: If Buyer fails to complete this purchase because of Buyer's default, Seller shall retain, as liquidated damages, the deposit actually paid. If the Property is a dwelling with no more than four units, one of which Buyer intends to occupy, then the amount retained shall be no more than 3% of the purchase price. Any excess shall be returned to Buyer. Release of funds will require mutual, Signed release instructions from both Buyer and Seller, judicial decision or arbitration award.**

BUYER AND SELLER SHALL SIGN A SEPARATE LIQUIDATED DAMAGES PROVISION FOR ANY INCREASED DEPOSIT. (C.A.R. FORM RID)

Buyer's Initials ________ / ________ **Seller's Initials** ________ / ________

17. **DISPUTE RESOLUTION:**

A. **MEDIATION:** Buyer and Seller agree to mediate any dispute or claim arising between them out of this Agreement, or any resulting transaction, before resorting to arbitration or court action. Paragraphs 17B(2) and (3) below apply to mediation whether or not the Arbitration provision is initialed. Mediation fees, if any, shall be divided equally among the parties involved. If, for any dispute or claim to which this paragraph applies, any party commences an action without first attempting to resolve the matter through mediation, or refuses to mediate after a request has been made, then that party shall not be entitled to recover attorney fees, even if they would otherwise be available to that party in any such action. THIS MEDIATION PROVISION APPLIES WHETHER OR NOT THE ARBITRATION PROVISION IS INITIALED.

B. **ARBITRATION OF DISPUTES: (1) Buyer and Seller agree that any dispute or claim in Law or equity arising between them out of this Agreement or any resulting transaction, which is not settled through mediation, shall be decided by neutral, binding arbitration, including and subject to paragraphs 17B(2) and (3) below. The arbitrator shall be a retired judge or justice, or an attorney with at least 5 years of residential real estate Law experience, unless the parties mutually agree to a different arbitrator, who shall render an award in accordance with substantive California Law. The parties shall have the right to discovery in accordance with California Code of Civil Procedure §1283.05. In all other respects, the arbitration shall be conducted in accordance with Title 9 of Part III of the California Code of Civil Procedure. Judgment upon the award of the arbitrator(s) may be entered into any court having jurisdiction. Interpretation of this agreement to arbitrate shall be governed by the Federal Arbitration Act.**

(2) EXCLUSIONS FROM MEDIATION AND ARBITRATION: The following matters are excluded from mediation and arbitration: (i) a judicial or non-judicial foreclosure or other action or proceeding to enforce a deed of trust, mortgage or installment land sale contract as defined in California Civil Code §2985; (ii) an unlawful detainer action; (iii) the filing or enforcement of a mechanic's lien; and (iv) any matter that is within the jurisdiction of a probate, small claims or bankruptcy court. The filing of a court action to enable the recording of a notice of pending action, for order of attachment, receivership, injunction, or other provisional remedies, shall not constitute a waiver of the mediation and arbitration provisions.

(3) BROKERS: Buyer and Seller agree to mediate and arbitrate disputes or claims involving either or both Brokers, consistent with 17A and B, provided either or both Brokers shall have agreed to such mediation or arbitration prior to, or within a reasonable time after, the dispute or claim is presented to Brokers. Any election by either or both Brokers to participate in mediation or arbitration shall not result in Brokers being deemed parties to the Agreement.

"NOTICE: BY INITIALING IN THE SPACE BELOW YOU ARE AGREEING TO HAVE ANY DISPUTE ARISING OUT OF THE MATTERS INCLUDED IN THE 'ARBITRATION OF DISPUTES' PROVISION DECIDED BY NEUTRAL ARBITRATION AS PROVIDED BY CALIFORNIA LAW AND YOU ARE GIVING UP ANY RIGHTS YOU MIGHT POSSESS TO HAVE THE DISPUTE LITIGATED IN A COURT OR JURY TRIAL. BY INITIALING IN THE SPACE BELOW YOU ARE GIVING UP YOUR JUDICIAL RIGHTS TO DISCOVERY AND APPEAL, UNLESS THOSE RIGHTS ARE SPECIFICALLY INCLUDED IN THE 'ARBITRATION OF DISPUTES' PROVISION. IF YOU REFUSE TO SUBMIT TO ARBITRATION AFTER AGREEING TO THIS PROVISION, YOU MAY BE COMPELLED TO ARBITRATE UNDER THE AUTHORITY OF THE CALIFORNIA CODE OF CIVIL PROCEDURE. YOUR AGREEMENT TO THIS ARBITRATION PROVISION IS VOLUNTARY."

"WE HAVE READ AND UNDERSTAND THE FOREGOING AND AGREE TO SUBMIT DISPUTES ARISING OUT OF THE MATTERS INCLUDED IN THE 'ARBITRATION OF DISPUTES' PROVISION TO NEUTRAL ARBITRATION."

Buyer's Initials ________ / ________ **Seller's Initials** ________ / ________

Buyer's Initials (________) (________)
Seller's Initials (________) (________)

Reviewed by __________ Date __________

Property Address: *560 La Mirada Drive Oakland, CA 94619* Date: *June 19, 2007*

18. PRORATIONS OF PROPERTY TAXES AND OTHER ITEMS: Unless otherwise agreed in writing, the following items shall be PAID CURRENT and prorated between Buyer and Seller as of Close Of Escrow: real property taxes and assessments, interest, rents, HOA regular, special, and emergency dues and assessments imposed prior to Close Of Escrow, premiums on insurance assumed by Buyer, payments on bonds and assessments assumed by Buyer, and payments on Mello-Roos and other Special Assessment District bonds and assessments that are now a lien. The following items shall be assumed by Buyer WITHOUT CREDIT toward the purchase price: prorated payments on Mello-Roos and other Special Assessment District bonds and assessments and HOA special assessments that are now a lien but not yet due. Property will be reassessed upon change of ownership. Any supplemental tax bills shall be paid as follows: **(i)** for periods after Close Of Escrow, by Buyer; and **(ii)** for periods prior to Close Of Escrow, by Seller. TAX BILLS ISSUED AFTER CLOSE OF ESCROW SHALL BE HANDLED DIRECTLY BETWEEN BUYER AND SELLER. Prorations shall be made based on a 30-day month.

19. WITHHOLDING TAXES: Seller and Buyer agree to execute any instrument, affidavit, statement or instruction reasonably necessary to comply with federal (FIRPTA) and California withholding Law, if required (C.A.R. Forms AS and AB).

20. MULTIPLE LISTING SERVICE ("MLS"): Brokers are authorized to report to the MLS a pending sale and, upon Close Of Escrow, the terms of this transaction to be published and disseminated to persons and entities authorized to use the information on terms approved by the MLS.

21. EQUAL HOUSING OPPORTUNITY: The Property is sold in compliance with federal, state and local anti-discrimination Laws.

22. ATTORNEY FEES: In any action, proceeding, or arbitration between Buyer and Seller arising out of this Agreement, the prevailing Buyer or Seller shall be entitled to reasonable attorney fees and costs from the non-prevailing Buyer or Seller, except as provided in paragraph 17A.

23. SELECTION OF SERVICE PROVIDERS: If Brokers refer Buyer or Seller to persons, vendors, or service or product providers ("Providers"), Brokers do not guarantee the performance of any Providers. Buyer and Seller may select ANY Providers of their own choosing.

24. TIME OF ESSENCE; ENTIRE CONTRACT; CHANGES: Time is of the essence. All understandings between the parties are incorporated in this Agreement. Its terms are intended by the parties as a final, complete and exclusive expression of their Agreement with respect to its subject matter, and may not be contradicted by evidence of any prior agreement or contemporaneous oral agreement. If any provision of this Agreement is held to be ineffective or invalid, the remaining provisions will nevertheless be given full force and effect. **Neither this Agreement nor any provision in it may be extended, amended, modified, altered or changed, except in writing Signed by Buyer and Seller.**

25. OTHER TERMS AND CONDITIONS, including attached supplements:

A. ☑ Buyer's Inspection Advisory (C.A.R. Form BIA)

B. ☒ Purchase Agreement Addendum (C.A.R. Form PAA paragraph numbers: *4A*) *secondary financing*

C. ☒ Statewide Buyer and Seller Advisory (C.A.R. Form SBSA)

D. *Seller shall have Property professionally cleaned after moving out and prior to COE.*

26. DEFINITIONS: As used in this Agreement:

A. **"Acceptance"** means the time the offer or final counter offer is accepted in writing by a party and is delivered to and personally received by the other party or that party's authorized agent in accordance with the terms of this offer or a final counter offer.

B. **"Agreement"** means the terms and conditions of this accepted California Residential Purchase Agreement and any accepted counter offers and addenda.

C. **"C.A.R. Form"** means the specific form referenced or another comparable form agreed to by the parties.

D. **"Close Of Escrow"** means the date the grant deed, or other evidence of transfer of title, is recorded. If the scheduled close of escrow falls on a Saturday, Sunday or legal holiday, then close of escrow shall be the next business day after the scheduled close of escrow date.

E. **"Copy"** means copy by any means including photocopy, NCR, facsimile and electronic.

F. **"Days"** means calendar days, unless otherwise required by Law.

G. **"Days After"** means the specified number of calendar days after the occurrence of the event specified, not counting the calendar date on which the specified event occurs, and ending at 11:59PM on the final day.

H. **"Days Prior"** means the specified number of calendar days before the occurrence of the event specified, not counting the calendar date on which the specified event is scheduled to occur.

I. **"Electronic Copy" or "Electronic Signature"** means, as applicable, an electronic copy or signature complying with California Law. Buyer and Seller agree that electronic means will not be used by either party to modify or alter the content or integrity of this Agreement without the knowledge and consent of the other.

J. **"Law"** means any law, code, statute, ordinance, regulation, rule or order, which is adopted by a controlling city, county, state or federal legislative, judicial or executive body or agency.

K. **"Notice to Buyer to Perform"** means a document (C.A.R. Form NBP), which shall be in writing and Signed by Seller and shall give Buyer at least 24 hours **(or as otherwise specified in paragraph 14C(4))** to remove a contingency or perform as applicable.

L. **"Repairs"** means any repairs (including pest control), alterations, replacements, modifications or retrofitting of the Property provided for under this Agreement.

M. **"Signed"** means either a handwritten or electronic signature on an original document, Copy or any counterpart.

N. **Singular and Plural** terms each include the other, when appropriate.

Buyer's Initials (________) (________)
Seller's Initials (________) (________)

Reviewed by ________ Date ________

EQUAL HOUSING OPPORTUNITY

Jonathan and J

Property Address: 560 La Mirada Drive Oakland, CA 94619 Date: June 19, 2007

27. **AGENCY:**

A. **DISCLOSURE:** Buyer and Seller each acknowledge prior receipt of C.A.R. Form AD "Disclosure Regarding Real Estate Agency Relationships."

B. **POTENTIALLY COMPETING BUYERS AND SELLERS:** Buyer and Seller each acknowledge receipt of a disclosure of the possibility of multiple representation by the Broker representing that principal. This disclosure may be part of a listing agreement, buyer-broker agreement or separate document (C.A.R. Form DA). Buyer understands that Broker representing Buyer may also represent other potential buyers, who may consider, make offers on or ultimately acquire the Property. Seller understands that Broker representing Seller may also represent other sellers with competing properties of interest to this Buyer.

C. **CONFIRMATION:** The following agency relationships are hereby confirmed for this transaction:
Listing Agent Professional Realty Company (Print Firm Name) is the agent of (check one): ☒ the Seller exclusively; or ☐ both the Buyer and Seller.
Selling Agent REThink Real Estate - T. Nelson & Assoc. (Print Firm Name) (if not same as Listing Agent) is the agent of (check one): ☒ the Buyer exclusively; or ☐ the Seller exclusively; or ☐ both the Buyer and Seller. Real Estate Brokers are not parties to the Agreement between Buyer and Seller.

28. **JOINT ESCROW INSTRUCTIONS TO ESCROW HOLDER:**

A. **The following paragraphs, or applicable portions thereof, of this Agreement constitute the joint escrow instructions of Buyer and Seller to Escrow Holder,** which Escrow Holder is to use along with any related counter offers and addenda, and any additional mutual instructions to close the escrow: 1, 2, 4, 12, 13B, 14E, 18, 19, 24, 25B and 25D, 26, 28, 29, 32A, 33 and paragraph D of the section titled Real Estate Brokers on page 8. If a Copy of the separate compensation agreement(s) provided for in paragraph 29 or 32A, or paragraph D of the section titled Real Estate Brokers on page 8 is deposited with Escrow Holder by Broker, Escrow Holder shall accept such agreement(s) and pay out from Buyer's or Seller's funds, or both, as applicable, the Broker's compensation provided for in such agreement(s). The terms and conditions of this Agreement not set forth in the specified paragraphs are additional matters for the information of Escrow Holder, but about which Escrow Holder need not be concerned. Buyer and Seller will receive Escrow Holder's general provisions directly from Escrow Holder and will execute such provisions upon Escrow Holder's request. To the extent the general provisions are inconsistent or conflict with this Agreement, the general provisions will control as to the duties and obligations of Escrow Holder only. Buyer and Seller will execute additional instructions, documents and forms provided by Escrow Holder that are reasonably necessary to close the escrow.

B. A Copy of this Agreement shall be delivered to Escrow Holder within 3 business days after Acceptance (or ☐ ____________________). Buyer and Seller authorize Escrow Holder to accept and rely on Copies and Signatures as defined in this Agreement as originals, to open escrow and for other purposes of escrow. The validity of this Agreement as between Buyer and Seller is not affected by whether or when Escrow Holder Signs this Agreement.

C. Brokers are a party to the escrow for the sole purpose of compensation pursuant to paragraphs 29, 32A and paragraph D of the section titled Real Estate Brokers on page 8. Buyer and Seller irrevocably assign to Brokers compensation specified in paragraphs 29 and 32A, respectively, and irrevocably instruct Escrow Holder to disburse those funds to Brokers at Close Of Escrow or pursuant to any other mutually executed cancellation agreement. Compensation instructions can be amended or revoked only with the written consent of Brokers. Escrow Holder shall immediately notify Brokers: **(i)** if Buyer's initial or any additional deposit is not made pursuant to this Agreement, or is not good at time of deposit with Escrow Holder; or **(ii)** if Buyer and Seller instruct Escrow Holder to cancel escrow.

D. A Copy of any amendment that affects any paragraph of this Agreement for which Escrow Holder is responsible shall be delivered to Escrow Holder within 2 business days after mutual execution of the amendment.

29. **BROKER COMPENSATION FROM BUYER:** If applicable, upon Close Of Escrow, **Buyer** agrees to pay compensation to Broker as specified in a separate written agreement between Buyer and Broker.

30. **TERMS AND CONDITIONS OF OFFER:**
This is an offer to purchase the Property on the above terms and conditions. All paragraphs with spaces for initials by Buyer and Seller are incorporated in this Agreement only if initialed by all parties. If at least one but not all parties initial, a counter offer is required until agreement is reached. Seller has the right to continue to offer the Property for sale and to accept any other offer at any time prior to notification of Acceptance. Buyer has read and acknowledges receipt of a Copy of the offer and agrees to the above confirmation of agency relationships. If this offer is accepted and Buyer subsequently defaults, Buyer may be responsible for payment of Brokers' compensation. This Agreement and any supplement, addendum or modification, including any Copy, may be Signed in two or more counterparts, all of which shall constitute one and the same writing.

Buyer's Initials (______)(______)
Seller's Initials (______)(______)

Reviewed by ______ Date ______

EQUAL HOUSING OPPORTUNITY

Jonathan and J

Property Address: 560 La Mirada Drive Oakland, CA 94619 Date: June 19, 2007

31. EXPIRATION OF OFFER: This offer shall be deemed revoked and the deposit shall be returned unless the offer is Signed by Seller and a Copy of the Signed offer is personally received by Buyer, or by Tara-Nicholle Nelson, who is authorized to receive it by 5:00 PM on the third Day after this offer is signed by Buyer (or, if checked, ☒ by June 19, 2007 (date), at 7:00 ☐ AM ☒ PM).

Date June 19, 2007
BUYER
Jonathan A. Buyer
(Print name)

Date June 19, 2007
BUYER
Jacqueline A. Buyer
(Print name)

707 Salsbury Lane, #11, San Leandro CA 94578
(Address)

32. BROKER COMPENSATION FROM SELLER:

A. Upon Close Of Escrow, **Seller** agrees to pay compensation to Broker as specified in a separate written agreement between Seller and Broker.

B. If escrow does not close, compensation is payable as specified in that separate written agreement.

33. ACCEPTANCE OF OFFER: Seller warrants that Seller is the owner of the Property, or has the authority to execute this Agreement. Seller accepts the above offer, agrees to sell the Property on the above terms and conditions, and agrees to the above confirmation of agency relationships. Seller has read and acknowledges receipt of a Copy of this Agreement, and authorizes Broker to deliver a Signed Copy to Buyer.

☐ (If checked) **SUBJECT TO ATTACHED COUNTER OFFER, DATED** ______

Date June 19, 2007
SELLER
Alexander A. Seller
(Print name)

Date June 19, 2007
SELLER
Beatrix A. Seller
(Print name)

560 La Mirada Drive, Oakland, CA 94619
(Address)

(____/____) (Initials) **CONFIRMATION OF ACCEPTANCE:** A Copy of Signed Acceptance was personally received by Buyer or Buyer's authorized agent on (date) June 19, 2007 at 6:45 ☐ AM ☒ PM. **A binding Agreement is created when a Copy of Signed Acceptance is personally received by Buyer or Buyer's authorized agent whether or not confirmed in this document. Completion of this confirmation is not legally required in order to create a binding Agreement; it is solely intended to evidence the date that Confirmation of Acceptance has occurred.**

SAMPLE

REAL ESTATE BROKERS:

A. Real Estate Brokers are not parties to the Agreement between Buyer and Seller.

B. Agency relationships are confirmed as stated in paragraph 27.

C. If specified in paragraph 2A, Agent who submitted the offer for Buyer acknowledges receipt of deposit.

D. **COOPERATING BROKER COMPENSATION:** Listing Broker agrees to pay Cooperating Broker **(Selling Firm)** and Cooperating Broker agrees to accept, out of Listing Broker's proceeds in escrow: **(i)** the amount specified in the MLS, provided Cooperating Broker is a Participant of the MLS in which the Property is offered for sale or a reciprocal MLS; or **(ii)** ☐ (if checked) the amount specified in a separate written agreement (C.A.R. Form CBC) between Listing Broker and Cooperating Broker.

Real Estate Broker (Selling Firm) REThink Real Estate - T. Nelson & Assoc. DRE Lic. # 01402955
By Tara-Nicholle Nelson DRE Lic. # 01402955 Date June 19, 2007
Address 560 Vernon Street City Oakland State CA Zip 94610
Telephone (510)910-6713 Fax (510)291-9715 E-mail taranicholle@yahoo.com

Real Estate Broker (Listing Firm) Professional Realty Company DRE Lic. # 01234567
By Raquel Realtor DRE Lic. # 12345678 Date June 19, 2007
Address 1314 Grand Avenue City Oakland State CA Zip 94611
Telephone (510)555-1212 Fax (510)555-2121 E-mail raquelrealtor@url.com

ESCROW HOLDER ACKNOWLEDGMENT:

Escrow Holder acknowledges receipt of a Copy of this Agreement, (if checked, ☒ a deposit in the amount of $ 5,500.00), counter offer numbers N/A and N/A
N/A , and agrees to act as Escrow Holder subject to paragraph 28 of this Agreement, any supplemental escrow instructions and the terms of Escrow Holder's general provisions.

Escrow Holder is advised that the date of Confirmation of Acceptance of the Agreement as between Buyer and Seller is June 19, 2006

Escrow Holder ABC Title Company Escrow # 1234566789
By Erika Simpson Date June 21, 2006
Address 109 Lakeshore Avenue; Oakland, CA; 94610
Phone/Fax/E-mail (510)555-2323/(510)555-3434/erikas@abctitlecompany.com
Escrow Holder is licensed by the California Department of ☐ Corporations, ☒ Insurance, ☐ Real Estate. License # 34567

(____/____) **REJECTION OF OFFER:** No counter offer is being made. This offer was reviewed and rejected by Seller on (Seller's Initials) ______ (Date)

THIS FORM HAS BEEN APPROVED BY THE CALIFORNIA ASSOCIATION OF REALTORS® (C.A.R.). NO REPRESENTATION IS MADE AS TO THE LEGAL VALIDITY OR ADEQUACY OF ANY PROVISION IN ANY SPECIFIC TRANSACTION. A REAL ESTATE BROKER IS THE PERSON QUALIFIED TO ADVISE ON REAL ESTATE TRANSACTIONS. IF YOU DESIRE LEGAL OR TAX ADVICE, CONSULT AN APPROPRIATE PROFESSIONAL.
This form is available for use by the entire real estate industry. It is not intended to identify the user as a REALTOR®. REALTOR® is a registered collective membership mark which may be used only by members of the NATIONAL ASSOCIATION OF REALTORS® who subscribe to its Code of Ethics.

 Published and Distributed by:
REAL ESTATE BUSINESS SERVICES, INC.
a subsidiary of the California Association of REALTORS®
525 South Virgil Avenue, Los Angeles, California 90020

Reviewed by ______ Date ______

RPA-CA REVISED 1/06 (PAGE 8 OF 8)

CALIFORNIA RESIDENTIAL PURCHASE AGREEMENT (RPA-CA PAGE 8 OF 8) Jonathan and J

Chapter 8

Selecting the Best Mortgage: Handy Mortgage Guide

To ease our minds and offer great financial advice when it comes to the mortgage side of buying, we turn to executive vice president and retail national sales manager of Wells Fargo, Brad Blackwell.

Piper: What are some financial no-no's when preparing to purchase a home?

Brad: From a financial standpoint, don't go into the home-buying process blindly.

Before you start house hunting, you need to know what your credit score is, as lenders look at this number very closely to determine whether or not you qualify for a mortgage. The higher your score, the better chances you have of securing a lower interest rate, and the lower your rate, the more buying power you have.

Far too many first-time home buyers enter the process by finding their "dream homes" and making offers, only to have their hopes crushed by a mortgage lenders who can't approve them for financing. Before you even pick up the newspaper's real estate section, find a reputable mortgage advisor and get a pre-approval. Many real estate agents won't even show properties to their clients unless they're pre-approved for financing. A pre-approval is different from pre-qualification in the fact that it's a commitment from a lender indicating that it will provide financing up to a certain amount.

A pre-approval is like having cash in hand. You know exactly what you can spend, so you and your agent aren't wasting time looking at properties out of your price range. Sellers typically take offers from pre-approved buyers more seriously, as they know there's less chance of a buyer's financing falling through.

> **Hot Tip:**
>
> "Avoid the 'dream home' trap. Many first-time buyers want to jump right into their ideal home: master suite with walk-in closets, three-car garage, professional-grade kitchen, and so on. In most cases, renters won't be able to afford the mortgage on that property right out of the gate. Your first home should be a first step that eventually leads to your dream home. Be realistic, and buy according to your ability—and comfort—to manage the mortgage on something smaller. Build equity and go from there."
>
> —Brad Blackwell, executive vice president and Retail National Sales Manager, Wells Fargo

Also, make sure you understand the terms of the mortgage you're considering. If it's an ARM, when will the loan "reset?" If so, when will it reset, how often will your payments change, and what's the most your payments can go to? Is it a negative amortizing ARM (often called Option ARMs), where the minimum monthly payment is less than the principal and interest amounts due. That shortfall is tacked on to the loan's principal balance, and, through time, you may end up owing more than your original mortgage amount, and if your local housing market hits a downturn, you may end up owing more than your home is worth.

Piper: How important is credit to the home-buying process?

Brad: Credit is, very simply, the ability to borrow money—or obtain goods and services—with the promise to repay the lender through time. The interest rate charged to extend credit is usually a reflection of the lender's confidence in the borrower's ability to repay. Credit is generally established by taking actions such as getting a credit card or auto loan, and paying back the money within the specified terms.

Your credit score is one of several things lenders look at when you're applying for a mortgage. It provides a snapshot of your financial history, and helps lenders determine if you're a good financial risk, how likely it will be that you'll repay the loan, and whether or not you qualify for their best interest rate.

Many people who have less-than-perfect credit are still able to find themselves in a position to qualify for mortgage financing. A reputable lender who has experience in working with customers with credit challenges can help you determine what mortgage options are available to you.

Above all, make sure you understand the terms of your loan, especially if there are prepayment penalties. After a year or two of making on-time mortgage payments, your credit score may improve to the point that you could refinance into a loan with a better interest rate, but you'll need to be aware of any prepayment penalties before doing so.

Piper: What are options for little or no money down when buying? What are some down-payment assistance programs?

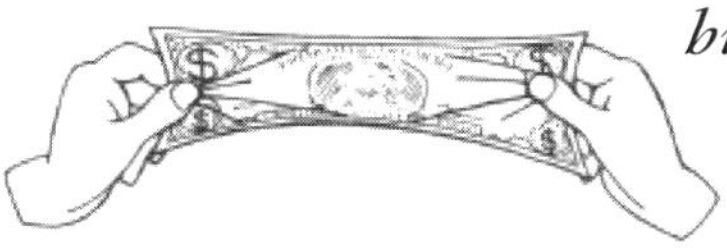

Brad: No- or little-money-down financing options have become more commonplace in the last several years. It is no longer necessary to wait until you have saved 20 percent of a home's value before you are able to buy a home. Recent research done by Wells Fargo Home Mortgage shows that 73 percent of recent first-time homebuyers had a down payment of 15 percent or less. Other data from the National Association of Realtors showed that during the height of the housing boom of 2004 and 2005, about four in 10 first-time buyers put nothing down.

While it's important to know that not having a large down payment is no longer a barrier for many first-time home buyers, it's also important to understand the risks associated with low or no down payment options.

When you make a down payment, you immediately have some equity in your home. That equity helps create a financial cushion for you and your family. During the last several years of strong appreciation growth, homeowners who put little to nothing down on

MONEY SAVER:

"Down payment assistance programs can vary greatly depending on the state, county and even city you're wanting to live in. The U.S. Department of Housing and Urban Development has a great resource page that can help potential buyers find programs by state at *http://hud.gov/buying*. A good mortgage consultant who works regularly with first-time home buyers should be able to help you find programs for which you're eligible. More and more of these programs require some sort of financial literacy education component in order to qualify, and even some financial institutions offer the same types of programs with the same requirements."

—Brad Blackwell, Wells Fargo

their property were able to build significant equity simply by living in the home for a short period of time, but the ability to take advantage of real estate appreciation is dependent on current market conditions where you live.

Piper: What are some tips for finding a great mortgage company?

Brad: Ask around and shop around. Talk to family, friends, coworkers—anyone who's bought at least one—if not more—homes. See who they'd recommend—and who they'd avoid. If one or two names consistently appear, that's likely a good place to start.

Don't overlook financial institutions you have relationships with, as they very often have special loan programs for their existing customers.

Above all else, you should feel comfortable with the mortgage consultant with whom you're working. They should be asking you questions to better understand what your needs are, what kind of loan you're comfortable with, and how this home fits in to your overall financial strategy. Conversely, they should be answering your questions satisfactorily. If they're being elusive, or trying to get you to take on a loan you're not comfortable with—don't be afraid to walk away.

Shop for a mortgage before you begin house hunting, and get that pre-approval letter from your lender. Knowing what you can spend before falling in love with your dream home not only helps you avoid the heartbreak of finding out you can't purchase it, it can prevent you from making a bad decision at the closing table.

Piper: What are the up-front fees/costs of home buying you should prepare for?

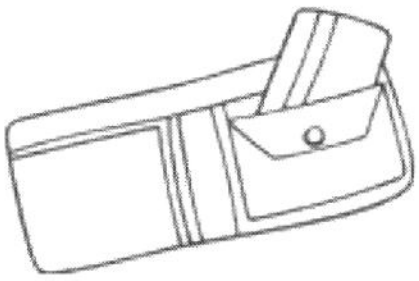

Brad: Fees can vary from lender to lender, and even from mortgage loan to mortgage loan, so it's difficult to say what types of fees consumers will encounter. Many of these costs are influenced by the size of your loan, so the larger the loan you receive, the higher the fees you typically pay. Several of these fees are actually paid to third parties, such as attorneys, property appraisers, and so on, so the lender may not have the flexibility over some of these fees that they may with others.

- Origination fees: Typically one to two percent of the loan amount, this is a fee the lender can also sometimes call "points." It's essentially a fee where you're prepaying some interest on the loan. Generally, loans where you pay points have lower interest rates, whereas loans with no points have slightly higher rates.

- Escrow fees: These cover the costs of preparing and sending all of documents and funds related to the purchase process.
- Title Insurance: This coverage is designed to protect both the borrower and the bank on the chance the seller doesn't actually own the home you're buying.
- Property Appraisal: To ensure the property you're buying meets their requirements, the lender will have a third-party appraiser estimate the value of the property.
- Property Insurance: Nearly every lender requires you to have homeowner's insurance on the property you're purchasing, and you'll typically need to have the policy in place and prepaid for the first year at the time of closing.
- Property Inspections: Both the lender and the property insurance company require inspections to ensure the property is structurally sound and free of problems such as termites, mold, water damage, and so on.
- Property Taxes: If the sellers have prepaid any property taxes on the property, you may have to reimburse them for the pro-rated amount.
- Private Mortgage Insurance (PMI): This insurance coverage is typically required by the lender if you have a down payment of less than 20 percent of the purchase price. It provides the lender some protection should you default on the loan and enter foreclosure. Once you hit the 20 percent equity threshold—through paying down the principal balance, and/or appreciation—you can typically have this fee removed by paying for another appraisal on your property that shows you've now got more than 20 percent equity.

Piper: Aside from credit, what are other factors that affect your ability to purchase a home?

Brad: During the approval process, lenders want and need to understand your complete financial situation. They'll look at what are commonly called the four Cs: *Capacity* (Income), *Character* (credit history), *Capital* (savings), and *Collateral* (the property you want to buy).

Piper: If you have average credit or poor credit and you decide to restore/improve your credit before your buy—how does this affect you?

Brad: Consumers with credit challenges can and do purchase homes everyday, so a few "dings" on your credit report won't necessarily mean you'll spend the rest of your life as a renter. But the better your credit score and financial situation, the better your chances of getting the best interest rate on your mortgage. So if you have credit challenges and you're still several months away from beginning the home buying process, you may have enough time to start improving your credit score and other aspects of your financial situation.

Piper: Do you have any other tips to save money when buying? Financial tips we rarely hear about, but should definitely know?

Brad: Ask your lender if they offer a bi-weekly mortgage drafting program, and consider taking advantage of it. With these programs, half of your monthly mortgage payment is automatically withdrawn from the bank account of your choice every two weeks. Over the course of a year, 26 drafts are equal to 13 monthly payments. That extra payment is applied toward your mortgage's outstanding principal balance, so you're paying down your loan faster and reducing your overall interest obligation to the lender.

For example: Let's assume you take out a $200,000, 30-year mortgage with a 6% interest rate. If you carry that loan the full term and only make the monthly payments, you'll have paid approximately $230,000 in interest. Using a bi-weekly drafting plan, you'll have the house paid off in about 25 years and shave approximately $48,000 from the total interest you paid on the loan.

If you're like most homeowners today, you won't live in the first home you buy 30 years from now, but there are still advantages to the program. Bi-weekly drafting lets you build equity in your home faster, so, if you do sell it in five to seven years, you've got more money for the down payment on your next home. It also helps you build and maintain your credit, while managing your monthly budget more effectively. Most people are paid every two weeks, and having half your mortgage payment drafted from your account automatically seems to help many people manage their cash flow better. Automatic drafting also means you'll never have to worry about forgetting to mail your mortgage payment in on time. For homeowners interested in rebuilding or maintaining their credit, that can help your efforts substantially.

Many lenders charge enrollment fees and drafting fees to use their program (Wells Fargo does not!), but even if you have to pay those fees, it can still save you money in the long run.

What Are Your Mortgage Options?

The fixed-rate mortgage and adjustable-rate mortgage (ARM) are the two most popular and widely used mortgages in the United States. *LowerMyBills.com* gives us a breakdown on fixed-rate mortgages, adjustable-rate mortgages (ARM), 40-, 45- and 50-year mortgages, two-step mortgage, interest-only ARMs, hybrid mortgage, and option ARM.

- 40-, 45- and 50-year mortgages: High housing costs have recently led to the availability of longer term, fully amortizing loans such as the 40-, 45-, or 50-year loan. These long-term loans have lower monthly payments, but the total cost is much higher than that of a 30-year mortgage, for instance, because payments are stretched out for up to two decades longer. These new long-terms loans may be an option for buyers who cannot qualify for other options. However, a borrower can typically afford "more house" with a 50-year loan than with a 30-year loan. A benefit of these loans is that the homeowner avoids negative amortization. On the downside, equity builds up at very slow rate.

- Two-step Mortgage: A two-step mortgage combines elements of fixed and adjustable-rate mortgages because it features a fixed rate and payment for an initial period, followed by one adjustment into a fixed rate for the remainder of the loan term. For example, a 7/23, has an initial fixed period of seven years, then 23 years of payments following the one rate adjustment.

Fixed-Rate Mortgage	Adjustable-Rate Mortgage
The fixed-rate mortgage is the more common of the two as it consists of fixed monthly interest rates—and therefore, set monthly payments—making it more stable and less risky than its cousin the ARM. Pros: o Homeowners borrow money on a long-term basis without having to worry about changes in interest rates impacting their monthly payments. o A consistent payment makes for easy budgeting over the life of the loan. o Can choose period of repayment ranging from 10 to 50 years. The 15- and 30-year terms are the most popular. o Lower risk loan. o Terms are easier to understand.	Unlike fixed-rate mortgages, the interest rate and monthly payments of an ARM loan are subject to fluctuating interest rates. Many have an initial fixed-rate period during which the borrower's rate doesn't change, followed by a much longer period during which the rate changes at preset intervals. Pros: o Offers lower interest rates and payments early in the term, enabling many consumers to become homeowners who couldn't otherwise afford the higher monthly payments of a fixed-rate loan. o In an environment when interest rates are declining, borrowers can take advantage of lower interest rates without having to refinance and pay related fees.

Cons: ○ Payment does not automatically adjust to take advantage of decreases in interest rates. While refinancing is an option, additional fees may be incurred. ○ Higher interest rates and monthly payments at the beginning of the loan. ○ May be too expensive for some borrowers, especially in a high interest rate environment. ○ May not be able to take advantage of long-term benefits. Most homeowners don't live in their home for the life of the loan. On average, Americans live in their homes fewer than 10 years.	○ A less-expensive and minimal risk option for homeowners who don't expect to live in their home for an extended period of time. ○ Homeowners who expect their income to grow can get into a house with more affordable, lower payments and have them increase as their income increases. Cons: ○ Interest rates and payments can increase significantly over the life of the loan in accordance with the economic environment. ○ On certain ARMs, called negative amortization loans, monthly payments are set very low to make the loan more affordable. However, they cover only a portion of the interest and any unpaid amount due is rolled into the principal balance. Borrowers can ultimately owe more money on the home than at closing. ○ Higher risk loan. ○ Terms can be difficult to understand. Borrowers should take care to understand the loan schedule and terms to be prepared when the loan adjusts and payments increase.

- Interest-only ARMs: Interest-only mortgages are gaining popularity with first-time home buyers. The reason for this is that interest-only ARMs offer great flexibility in terms of payments for the first several years of the loan. With an interest-only loan, the homeowner is actually only making payments on the interest of the loan, so the payment is substantially lower. Payments can be made toward the principal but are not required. After a set period of time, the loan adjusts to the current interest rate, after which the loan amortizes at a faster rate. Interest-only ARMs may be a good option for homeowners with fluctuating monthly expenses, such as those with commission-based salaries.
- Hybrid Mortgage: One-year ARMs, which have their first adjustment after one year, used to be the most popular adjustable. However, more common now is the hybrid loan, which combines a lengthy fixed period with a long adjustable period. The 5/1 ARM for example, has an initial fixed-rate period of five years after which the rate is adjusted annually thereafter. Other popular hybrid ARMs are the 3/1, the 7/1, and the 10/1.
- Option ARM: Option ARMs provide the homeowner with payment flexibility, making it an option for borrowers not on a set income, such as the self-employed. The option ARM offers four payment options each month so that payments are made based on the borrower's financial situation at payment time. Borrowers can pay the minimum payment, pay on the interest only (called negative amortization), pay towards principal and interest, or make an accelerated payment to pay off the loan more rapidly. This loan option is best for those comfortable with some risk in exchange for flexibility.

How to Apply for a Mortgage

Five Things Not to Forget in Your Mortgage Application

Filling out mortgage applications might be overwhelming but with some preparation, potential homeowners can minimize frustration. Before meeting with a lender, *LowerMyBills.com* says to be prepared with the following:

1. Residence history: Where have you lived over the past few years and did you rent or own? This is reflected on your credit report in most cases but lenders will want to know how long you have lived in a given location, if you rented, and so on, so they can make sure you are a viable credit risk.
2. History of employment: One way a lender determines the legitimacy of the borrower is by looking at employment history. Consumers consistently employed at a given salary for a good period of time present a more viable credit risk.
3. What are your assets?: Collateral can be a big piece of whether or not a consumer gets a loan. Do you have a car? Bank accounts? An IRA? All of these will affect your ability to get a home mortgage.
4. Credit history: Know your credit score and exactly what is on your credit report before filling out a mortgage application. Your credit report will be pulled and it's best to be familiar with it and explain any items if necessary.
5. An account of your expenses and payments: Calculations are done to determine what you can really afford. Rather than trying to lie to get more house than your budget can handle, let your lender be the guide on what is feasible for your budget.

Three Quick Steps to Completing a Mortgage Application Online

Filling out a mortgage application online may seem very easy. The truth is that no mortgage application, in person or online, is ever that simple so here are some tips to make the process easier.

1. Prepare: Get all the needed information together ahead of time. Have last year's taxes on hand, a pay stub, a bank statement, current creditors, and account information. Be prepared and the arduous part of mortgage application completion will be much quicker.
2. Find the site(s): Determine which lender Website to use before completing a mortgage application. Be cautious about completing multiple mortgage applications online so as to avoid giving your personal information to the wrong site. Consider a Website such as *www.lowermybills.com*, where after supplying some basic information, you will be matched with multiple lenders competing for your business.
3. Be thorough: Don't skip steps or leave items blank when filling out a mortgage application. Be precise and be thorough and the whole process will be better as a result.

Source: *LowerMyBills.com*

Options Jf You Don't Have Enough for Closing Costs

LowerMyBills.com provides what to do if you don't have enough money for closing costs or down payments. What are your options? Let's find out:

⇨ **Full doc versus stated doc:** Borrowers on a fixed income rather than commission- or tips-based for example, should opt for full doc (documentation) rather than stated doc when applying for a mortgage. With a full doc loan the borrower provides supporting documents (that is, W2s, pay stubs) to as proof of income. Full doc loans offer the better interest rate.

⇨ **Bi-weekly mortgage payments:** Some lenders allow homeowners to pay half of their mortgage payment every two weeks rather than monthly (this is different than making a payment twice per month). The payment plan pays off the principal more rapidly because you've paid off your yearly obligation in 48 weeks, so the other four weeks of payments go toward your principal. This reduces overall interest and pays off the loan sooner. Of course, borrowers should check with their lender prior to doing so.

⇨ **Public programs:** First-time home buyers in particular should explore public programs—typically sponsored by state, county, or city governments—that may offer better interest rates and terms than private lenders. Depending on the program and eligibility requirements, borrowers may be eligible for down payment assistance or a first-time home owner grant program. Contact state, county, and city housing agencies to see what they have to offer.

Hot Tip:

If you're on a shoestring budget, what advice do you have for folks?

- Comparison shop. Consumers looking to get into the housing market should check rates with different lenders and mortgage brokers to ensure they are getting the best deal. Websites like *LowerMyBills.com* allow consumers to get quotes from multiple lenders who then compete for the business with lower rates.
- Potential homeowners should know the prevailing interest rate for someone of their credit standing. The Internet is a great source for researching up-to-date rates.
- During the loan process, be wary of unnecessary or inflated fees, such as document preparation. Question unexplained or unusual fees.
- Some real estate companies offer home buyer rebates in which the buyer receives a rebate for a portion of the purchase price.

⇨ **Specialized programs:** Potential home buyers can look into public programs that offer loans with low interest rates or other incentives.

- Veterans Administration (VA) Loans.
- Federal Housing Administration (FHA) Loans.
- Teachers' programs.
- First-time home buyer programs.
- Fannie Mae home purchase programs.

MONEY SAVER:

How do the 20-80 loans or 100 percent full-financing (with no PMI) in some cases options work? Are there different variations of this, what are the pros and cons?

LowerMyBills.com: Most lenders require private mortgage insurance (PMI) of borrowers who put down less than 20 percent as protection against losses should the borrower default on the loan.

A potential homeowner should put down 20 percent of the purchase price as a down payment for several reasons. First, it eliminates the cost of PMI entirely. Second, it lowers the monthly payment (because less has been financed). Third, it allows the borrower to buy "more house" because the money that would have been for PMI now goes towards the mortgage payment.

In some situations, PMI may be avoided by taking out a second mortgage at the time of the home's purchase. These loans are called a 20-80 or "piggyback" loan. For example, the first mortgage would be for 80% of the purchase price (no PMI), the second mortgage for the amount needed to put 20 percent down in cash. In this way PMI payment is avoided, but there are potential downsides:

1. The second will be at a higher rate than the first mortgage.
2. Because the second mortgage may have a variable rate, the payment can increase over the term of the loan.
3. The second mortgage may have a balloon payment, meaning that the new balance may become due before the first mortgage is paid off.

One advantage to 20-80 loans is it allows the borrower to avoid PMI, which unlike interest on a loan, is not tax deductible.

The interest rate on a loan financing 100 percent of the borrower's home value is notably higher than financing 80 percent of the home, for example.

⇨ **Tap into an IRA:** The federal government allows for a one-time withdrawal, up to $10,000, from an IRA or retirement account with no penalty for first-time homebuyers.

⇨ **401(k) withdrawal:** In general, money in a 401(k) plans should stay there until retirement, however the IRS allows "hardship withdrawals" and one such hardship is a down payment for purchase of a primary residence. Borrowers should keep in mind that they are subject to taxes and penalties on the amount withdrawn due the year of the withdrawal.

⇨ **Borrow against a 401(k):** A second option may be to borrow against a 401(k) account. But beware—a homeowner who borrows against a 401(k) and loses his or her job or changes employers is obligated to pay back the loan in full within a short period of time. If not, the loan is treated as a withdrawal and subject to the same taxes and penalties as withdrawing from a 401(k). While 401(k) accounts can be rolled over into a new account or IRA, this is not the case with a loan against a 401(k).

Hot Tip:

"All first-time home buyers have many options. Some of these options are available from the lenders with zero-down financing to down-payment-assistance programs offered from different municipalities. If you don't have enough money for the closing costs you need to discuss this with your Realtor and try to get assistance from the seller to contribute towards those costs, most lenders will allow three to six percent seller concession for closing costs. Some programs will allow you to receive a gift from family members to help pay for down payment of closing costs. All of these options depends on the programs. Once again, it is essential to work with a mortgage professional that is going to look at your situation as a whole and do a mortgage plan not just a loan."

—Jonathan Shapiro, American Home Lenders, Inc.

⇨ **Gifts:** About 20 percent of first-time home buyers obtain money from parents, other relatives, or friends to go towards the down payment. It's not unheard of to request cash gifts for a "house account" in lieu of wedding gifts.

Chapter 9

Why Home Inspections Will Save You Money: Getting Repairs Done (But Not at Your Expense)

Home inspector Reggie Marston was examining a small ranch when he noticed a rake with a broken handle leaning against the wall under the kitchen sink window. It had been leaning there so long grass had grown up around the rake. He thought that for some reason the rake looked out of place. When he tugged the rake free, he realized why the rake had been strategically placed under the window. The owner of Residential Equity Management Home Inspections says, "The kitchen sink drain had clogged and instead of repairing the drain, the owner had rerouted the pipe through the wall to the outside and just let the sink and garbage disposal drain into a hole that was dug under the kitchen window. He had placed the rake there to cover the pipe protruding out of the wall."

Home inspectors see it all, even when sellers sometimes try to hide problems. Another inspector shared how he was inspecting a home when he found a huge hole in the wall hidden behind a painting of Jesus' Last Supper. There is another story out of Ohio in which a radiator hose was used as a pipe.

Home inspections are essential. Whether it's an old charming home or brand new construction, you'll want to be aware of defects unseen to your eyes. Make sure your contract is contingent on a home inspection, giving you the right to an inspection, as well as terms and conditions in dealing with what is discovered in the inspection. The contract will usually specify how many days you have to get it done. If you miss the deadline, you waive your right to a home inspection.

What's a Home Inspection?

A home inspection is a visual examination of a home prior to closing that determines if there are any visible major defects. The inspection should include the roof, basement, foundation, heating, cooling, plumbing, fireplace, attic, insulation, doors, windows, interior, exterior, and crawlspace. In many cases, buyers use the home inspection to negotiate repairs, fix safety or maintenance issues, correct environmental hazards, and address other problems. American Society of Home Inspectors 2006 president Joe Corsetto says an inspector looks at the entire building from the roof to foundations—and everything in-between. Corsetto says, "To think as a home inspector does, divide the building into three major categories: exterior, interior, and major system components."

> **Hot Tip:**
> "The purpose of the exterior inspection is to identify those things that affect the building's exterior 'skin' and its ability to shed water or to be weather tight."
>
> —Joe Corsetto

Inspectors also inspect major system components such as plumbing, heating/cooling, mechanical components, electrical, and framing support system. Corsetto says, "Home inspections provide home buyers with an understanding of the condition of the major system components and if there is a concern that affects reliability or functional aspects of its operation."

Here's what happens in a home inspection:

1. The buyer will typically set up and pay for the home inspection. (Try to set it up early.)
2. The inspector will disclose visible defects in an inspection report and as you walk the home with him.
3. You may opt to present the seller with a list of repair requests.
4. You and the seller will negotiate.

EXTERIOR	INTERIOR
☑ Roof system ☑ Siding, cladding, trim ☑ Windows, doors ☑ Walks, steps, decks ☑ Property grading to the foundation ☑ Garage, carport (just to name a few) Source: Corsetto	☑ Inside, the focus shifts toward building areas that commonly allow water entry, such as: roof leakage, window/door frames and under floor areas below entry doors. ☑ Areas with wood-to-soil contact, which is an attraction for wood-destroying insects and wood rot/decay conditions. ☑ Functional aspects of baths, kitchens, interior living spaces, attic spaces, and whether the building structure is affecting these areas in a significant way. Each system or component is checked for operation or physical condition.

The negotiation may be to either get some or all of the repairs done, for the seller to credit repair costs at closing, or to try use it as leverage to reduce the home's price to cover the cost of repairs. Sometimes, if you feel there is too much damage, you may opt to walk away from the purchase and have your earnest money refunded. Other times, if the seller is selling the home "as-is," they may not be willing to make repairs. (But state laws vary and sometimes an "as-is" clause may not limit the seller's responsibilities.) It all depends on the situation.

Nicole Smith of RE/MAX Masters Broker-Associate Texas had this advice on negotiating repairs.

Piper: Should you go with credits or get the seller to do repairs?

Smith: Any time a buyer accepts a home with identified defects, there is a significant risk that the items will never be addressed correctly. I encourage the buyers I represent to ask the seller to hire qualified professionals to address all requested repairs prior to closing. This answer also completely depends upon each situation.

Piper: When do you recommend a buyer accepting a credit in lieu of repairs?

Smith: The only time I recommend a buyer accepting a credit in lieu of repairs is if the repairs aren't that significant to the overall integrity of the property *and* if the buyer prefers to do the repairs themselves. At that point, I call a handyman (or two) in our area who specializes in this type of repair. I ask them to provide a quote detailing what it would cost to address each item. Some estimates are within a range: $50 to repair; $100 plus parts to replace. The highest price is used to determine the total amount of the quote. In negotiating with the seller, the buyers I represent usually bump that number to compensate them for the inconvenience of managing the repairs and to also give them some room to negotiate.

In Texas, lenders don't like to see "credit in lieu of repairs" because it raises questions in the underwriters mind about the integrity of the property securing the loan they're approving. Therefore, the best way to handle a credit for repairs is to simply call it "seller credit toward buyer closing costs." In this way, even though it's not a check from the seller directly, it's less money that the buyer has to bring to closing, so it accomplishes the same goal. Further, this agreement is in writing, enforceable, and flows through the settlement statement with lender approval.

Piper: How do you ensure repairs get done?

Smith: When repairs are requested, I am very specific in my request that licensed providers render the service (to avoid the inevitable brother-in-law type fixes and future problems). I request receipts from all providers well in advance of the closing. The buyer and I do a walk-through prior to closing to ensure the work has been done. If it hasn't been done as contracted, then we attempt to resolve the issue immediately with the seller. Again, depending on the nature of the repair, we would either delay closing to allow for the repair to be completed or the buyer would accept a credit in lieu of that repair.

> **SHOESTRING TIP:**
>
> Another option is to ask the inspector to come back for a follow-up evaluation of the repairs that were made.

Need an Inspector?

It is simple. Word of mouth is the best form of recommendation. Ask your friends, family, coworkers, and neighbors for recommendations. If you ask your Realtor, have him suggest several candidates you can interview and select from. Be sure your inspector is certified with a national organization, such as the American Society of Home Inspectors (*www.ashi.org*), National Association of Certified Home Inspectors (*www.nachi.org*), or National Association of Home Inspectors (*www.nahi.org*). When you visit these sites, check out their Standards of Practice, to see the guidelines these inspectors adhere to. On each of these sites, you can search for a certified inspector in your hometown.

For example, we went to *www.ashi.org* to find an inspector and typed: Long Island, New York. At the time, it pulled up 39 ASHI certified inspectors in the area. It gave us the inspector's name, company name, and contact information. And, it literally took less than a minute. You can also specify additional criteria or specialties and search by name, zip code, area code, or major metro area.

To start your search for an inspector, or to check if the inspector you hired is certified, here is the contact information for the three leading national home inspection associations:

1. American Society of Home Inspectors, Inc. (ASHI)
   932 Lee Street, Suite 101
   Des Plaines, Illinois 60016.
   Website: *www.ashi.org*.
   Phone: 1-800-743-ASHI (2744).
2. National Association of Certified Home Inspectors (NACHI)
   1750 30th Street
   Boulder, Colorado 80301.
   Website: *www.nachi.org*.
   E-mail: FastReply@nachi.org.
3. National Association of Home Inspectors, Inc. (NAHI)
   4248 Park Glen Road
   Minneapolis, Minnesota 55416
   Website: *www.nahi.org*.
   Phone: (952) 928-4641 or (800) 448-3942.
   Fax: (952) 929-1318.
   E-mail: info@nahi.org.

Jnspecting Your Jnspector

We asked inspectors across the country: How do you find a quality inspector? Across the board, they recommended interviewing inspectors before selecting one. The price of the inspection shouldn't be the deciding factor. These are the questions inspectors say you should ask when searching for a quality inspector:

1. How many years have you been in the profession?
2. Are you affiliated with an association?
3. What was your previous profession?
4. What training did you receive to become an inspector?

> **Insiders Insight**
>
> "The search for a home inspector should start months before the inspection will be needed. The purchaser doesn't want to find a home, submit a contract, have the contract ratified with a home inspection within 3 to 7 days or they lose the right to an inspection. That time frame is not going to give them the opportunity to find a qualified home inspector, especially if the market is busy. The purchasers are probably going to find themselves hiring the first inspector that is available and that inspector may or may not be best qualified. As with all professions in the home inspection business, you've got the good, the bad and the real bad."
>
> —Reggie Marston, President, Northern Virginia Chapter of ASHI and Owner, Residential Equity Management Home Inspections

5. Are you familiar with the type of house you will be inspecting?
6. If you're new, will an experienced inspector be helping you?
7. Are you specifically trained in residential inspections?

> ***Hot Tip:***
>
> "The purchaser should not have to find themselves in a position where they have to obtain the names of home inspectors from anyone with a vested interest in the property (the owner, Realtors, lenders, appraisers). If they do, I would highly recommend that they get a list of names, not just one or two. Some of these organizations have what they call preferred provider lists. These lists are composed of companies that have paid a fee to be on the list. Being on the list doesn't necessarily mean that they're qualified. Sometimes people with a vested interest in the sale proceeding smoothly won't provide the purchaser with the name of the most thorough inspector in the area."
>
> —Reggie Marston, Owner, Residential Equity Management Home Inspections

It's also important that you see an example of the inspector's home inspection report so you get an idea of what yours will look like when you receive it. There is no standard for home inspection reports, so be sure the sample report you see is legible and easy to understand, because that's what yours will resemble. Inspector Marston says you should also inquire about "professional affiliations, insurances, contracts, references, Better Business Bureau, reports, request referrals, [and] lastly, check about price, but don't make the decision based on price."

Horror story

"A good example of where a home inspector did a poor job is the Clemon's house in Longwood, Florida. The house was wood frame with stucco below grade. There was no mention of this made in the inspection report. A few months after moving in, they noticed termites swarming in several areas. This led them to investigate further and do some destructive probing. They found termite damage throughout the home. They called the county building department to come out and take a look at it.

SHOESTRING TIP:

What should you look for in an inspector? "Ethics is the main quality you should look for in an inspector. Be sure your real estate agent isn't being paid to recommend the inspector to you (preferred vendor list) and make sure the inspector is a member of an association that prohibits its members from offering repair services. There are three associations that correctly prohibit this unconscionable practice: NACHI (*www.nachi.org*), ASHI (*www.ashi.org*), and MICB at (*www.certifiedmasterinspector.org*)."

—Nick Gromicko, Founder, National Association of Certified Home Inspectors, *www.nachi.org*.

"The county condemned the house and gave them three hours to get their possessions out. Because their inspector did not do his job, they are out $100,000 in cash and they have a $500,000 mortgage on a useless house."

—Greg Bell, owner, Bell Inspection Service

Hot Tip:

Common Causes of Building Damage

"Water penetration and wood-destroying insects/organisms account for common causes of building damage. If severe enough, water penetration can result in conditions that can negatively affect indoor air quality and building habitability."

—Joe Corsetto, former ASHI President and Owner of Shelterworks,Inc., Dover, New Jersey

Do You Need to Attend the Jnspection?

You don't have to, but wouldn't you like to know what defects the inspector finds in your prospective home? If the inspector or agent tries to discourage you from attending, this should be a red flag. Home inspections typically take two to four hours. Ask the inspector how long he estimates it will take to do the home inspection. RE/MAX Masters Broker-Associate Smith says, "It is very important to get the home inspected under every circumstance—even if it is a brand new home or belongs to someone you know and trust."

ERA Realtor Teddy Goodson, ABR, CRS, who has been in real estate since 1967, says, "My view is that the home inspection is supposed to provide the buyer with an understanding of what he is buying, the features and idiosyncrasies of his new home, an education in how to maintain it, and a disclosure of any serious defects not readily apparent to the eye, which might be a matter of safety or very expensive to fix. In other words, unknown booby traps."

U.S. Inspect shares with us common repair/replacement cost estimates:

Repair/Replacement Items	Cost Projections*
Replace metal chimney flashings and roof valleys, each side.	$275–350 per item
Regrade ground surface to divert surface water. Average home, 30–40'.	$600–1,200 ($20–30/LF)
Upgrade electric service to 200 amps; includes new service cable and main distribution panel (no additional wiring or circuits).	$1,100–1,500 LS
Install 20-year, standard fiberglass reinforced asphalt composition shingles. Average home, 1,500 SF roof. Removal of existing shingles not included.	$2,500–3,500
Replace standard gas-fired, forced air heating unit. Average home, approximately 100,000 BTU input.	$1,800–2,600
Repair concrete block foundation wall. Average conditions, 30 LF wall.	$4,500–6,000 ($150-200/LF)
Remove and replace concrete foundation wall. Average conditions, 30 LF wall.	$9,000–10,500
Replaced failed chimney lining. Average two-story home. Average difficulty; stainless steel.	$1,500–2,000
Treatment of soil for termites. Average home. Average difficulty.	$700–900
Remove ceramic tile and damaged substrate. Install water-proof substrate and new tile in damaged area only.	$300–400
Replace pipe from septic tank to distribution box.	$250–350
Replace septic tank.	$1,500–2,000
Replace drainage/leaching fields	$6,000–20,000

* (LF = linear feet, LS = lump sum, SF = square feet)

Source: *USInspect.com*

Spotting Hidden Defects

Home inspector Greg Bell, owner of Bell Inspection Service, says there is no way to spot hidden defects. But, he says, "What we do look for are signs that could lead to there being hidden defects." While nothing beats the fine-tuned eye of a home inspector, Bell points out red flags you can look out for when inspecting your home.

Red flags:

- Electrical items to look for:
  - Electrical panels: Federal Pacific and Zinsco. Look at the panel to see who is the manufacturer. Bell says, "These two manufacturers have a history of problems with their panels. That is why you should look for them."

  - Wiring: Aluminum wiring was installed in some homes for the early 1960s until 1974. Any home built during this time period has the potential of having this material used for the general household circuits.
  - Outlets: Check any outlets around a water source to ensure they are GFCI protected. GFCI is Ground Fault Circuit Interrupter. This will shut off the circuit if you were to drop your hair dryer in the sink or bathtub.
- Plumbing:
  - Homes built before 1970: These may have tar and paper material used for the main drain line. This material is at the end of its designed life. When it fails, it will collapse causing waste water to back up into the home. A good way to determine if it has been replaced is to look for PVC clean out.

Hot Tip:

What is a PVC clean out?

"A clean out provides access to the sewer drain if needed to clean it out. It can be found on the outside of the home usually within five feet of the exterior."

—Greg Bell

- PB Piping: This is another problem that is easily identified. It is the gray pipe that has brass or copper rings clamped at the joints. PB pipe is the material used to provide water for the whole house. Visit *www.pbpipe.com* for more information.
- Septic tank: Does the home have a septic tank? Tip: Get a septic contractor to pump the tank so it can be properly inspected. Many inspectors offer a dye test for the septic system, but check to find out if this service is included in the basic home inspection or if a septic inspection includes an additional fee.

Interior:

- Door openings/windows: Make sure everything is square.
- Water stains: Look for any water stains in the ceiling and inside cabinets that are in wet locations.

Exterior:

- Roof: Look for flashing along the roof line.
- On a wood-frame house: Make sure stucco is above grade. Stucco below grade allows termites to go undetected until major damage has occurred.

—Greg Bell, Bell Inspection Service. He is a certified inspector with the National Association of Certified Home Inspectors and founder of the Central Florida Chapter of NACHI

MONEY SAVER

Small Problems, Future Nightmares

How to catch a small problem while it's small—before it costs you big time.

- Problem: Water-related concerns can start out small and blossom into significant repairs with wood rot/decay and mold, says Joe Corsetto.

☑ Repair: He says, sometimes, "simple exterior caulking, maintenance, and painting can prevent extensive wall cavity damage to the building structure."

- Problem: Heating system maintenance. Corsetto says, "Poor maintenance can lead to breakdown and failure to operate or worse." He says if your area is prone to below-freezing temperatures and your heating system stops working you may suffer from no heat, plumbing damage, and pipe failure that leads to more problems. Corsetto says, "Lack of heating system maintenance, which includes evaluation for proper venting, can also lead to exhaust gas leakage and carbon monoxide poisoning in extreme cases."

☑ Repair: Maintain the heating system.

The home has so much damage you no longer want it. What are your options?

Q & A

I spoke with home inspector Dan Osborn of Upstate Home Inspection Service in Upstate New York for tips for buyers in the home inspection process.

Piper: What are some hidden defects buyers should be aware of?

Dan: Moisture is the enemy of the house. The most important aspect of maintaining the house is to keep water out of it with a good roof, good gutters, proper grading and drainage, proper handling of moisture in

MONEY SAVER

The home has so much damage you no longer want it, what are your options?

"This is totally dependent on the contract that was negotiated between the buyer and the seller. Our board contract requires that the buyer identify the issues, make requests for repairs, and give the seller the opportunity to make the repairs. Other contracts give the buyer the option to cancel the contract."

—Linda Davis,
RE/MAX Realty Group, Connecticut.

the basement and proper drainage and use of sump pumps. I call all these systems a "water management system" which encompasses every area of the house. It's the moisture that causes, mold, rot, termites, and so on.

Piper: Why do home inspections save you money in the long run?

Dan: Home inspectors will hopefully find the problems with a house, but more than that, they will give you advice on how to maintain a house through time so that you can keep the small problems small before they become big ones. Best example of that is proper venting of an attic. It might cost $200 for an attic fan, or you can replace that 20-year roof you just had installed after only 12 years because it cooked from underneath or because you didn't install a ridge vent.

Piper: What should every potential home buyer know?

Dan: There is always another house. Don't make a $200,000 decision on a house based on how close the house is to a school or the mall. This decision to buy the house is first, and ultimately, a business decision and should not be made by the heart.

Piper: What services does a good inspector offer?

Dan: The best thing a good home inspector can offer is a clear and concise explanation of the issues. We all look at the same things, yet how we convey that information might make the buyer run away because we scared him, or the buyer wasn't worried when he should have been. It is all in how the inspector communicates with the buyer. A buyer should always interview the inspector before hiring him to see if he likes the way he talks and feels comfortable with the way an inspector communicates.

Piper: What should you know about environmental hazards/ toxins?

Dan: Mold, fungus, radon, asbestos, and lead are all things that can harm people. Inspectors should know how to spot them and when to call in an expert. Unless they have special expertise or certification, they should not try to be an expert on any of it; just recognizing the hazard is enough.

Piper: When you get a list of repairs that need to get done, what should you not avoid?

Dan: Any of the repairs that have to do with water infiltration, moisture levels, humidity, or ventilation. These are the issues that create mold and these are the most important issues that will create the most trouble over time.

The Seller Did a Pre-Inspection, Should You Do One, Too?

"Absolutely," says Joe Corsetto. "The focus here is on an independent opinion of the building condition. I suggest all purchasers acquire an independent evaluation of the building before they buy it."

Pre-listing home inspection completed for a seller "does not necessarily reflect the same concerns a buyer needs to address to make an informed purchase decision," says Corsetto. "Homeowners should acquire an independent home inspection performed by someone who works for them."

> ***Hot Tip:***
>
> **Disclosures**
>
> Most states require sellers to let buyers know all known problems with the house (structural, mechanica,l and legal), plus disclosures for lead paint and other hazards. (If your home is built before 1978, you should receive a lead disclosure form.)
>
> —*The For Sale by Owner Handbook* (Career Press, 2005)

Finding a Compromise

"A buyer was purchasing his first house, which was a nice solidly built home that needed updating and cosmetic repairs. As expected, there were a number of issues in the home inspection. One of the unexpected issues identified was the age of the furnace, which was working properly, but raised some concerns with the home inspector. Although both the buyer and the seller were reasonable folks, the seller was unwilling to pay for a new furnace along with the other repairs necessary. The buyer had planned to budget for a new furnace, along with new appliances, but hoped to have at least a year or two to save. They became concerned that if everything needed replacement sooner than expected, they would find themselves in a financial position they had not anticipated. With the advice of their agent (me), the seller offered the buyer a one year home warranty. This made the buyers feel comfortable about any unexpected repairs during the first year." —Linda Davis, Realtor, RE/MAX Realty Group

Termite Inspections

When Steve found out from a termite inspection that the home's structure was destroyed by termites, he decided not to buy it. Getting the termite inspection done and treating any termite issues typically falls in the hands of the seller. U.S. Inspect says a termite inspection is a visual inspection of a home's interior (including basements and crawlspaces) and exterior for evidence of wood-destroying insects (WDI) and wood-destroying organisms (WDO). In areas where drywood termites are an issue, the attic may also be inspected. A report is drawn up and is given to the seller to resolve the problems. For example, in one instance, a termite inspection exposed termite damage to the front porch railing and a beehive in the attic. The seller had to get the problems resolved and have receipts proving it had been fixed for the buyer's mortgage lender.

Other Jnspections You Can Get

You can get specialized inspections in addition to a whole house inspection. For example, a buyer could get a chimney inspection because of worries about a crack found in the chimney. Among common additional inspections are termite inspections, chimney inspections, sewer, and underground storage tanks. U.S. Inspect shares with us a list of inspections available to you (aside from just the standard home inspection).

- ☑ Radon Testing: Radon, the second leading cause of lung cancer, is a radioactive gas emitted from the ground that may seep into the home.
- ☑ Chimney: Chimney specialists evaluate the overall condition of a chimney. Annually after you move in, have a chimney sweep clean and inspect your chimney to ensure its safety.
- ☑ Electrical: Electrical specialists evaluate the overall condition of a home's electrical system.
- ☑ Geotechnical: Geotechnical engineers analyze soil to determine its stability.
- ☑ Heating, Ventilation, and Air Conditioning: HVAC specialists evaluate the overall condition of a home heating, ventilation, and air conditioning system.
- ☑ Lead Paint: Lead paint specialists perform a noninvasive inspection to determine the presence of lead in paint.
- ☑ Plumbing: Plumbing specialists evaluate the overall condition of a home's plumbing system.
- ☑ Pool/Hot Tub: Pool and hot tub specialists evaluate the overall condition and operability of the system and/or components of a swimming pool, hot tub, spa, or Jacuzzi.
- ☑ Roof.
- ☑ Seawall: Dock and seawall specialists evaluate the condition of a home's dock and seawall.

☑ Septic Dye: Septic system specialists use a tracer dye to determine current surface breakout in a system—a cursory check of a septic system's operability.

☑ Underground Storage Tank: Underground storage tank (UST) specialists perform soil or tightness tests to determine the integrity of a UST and its fuel and vent lines.

☑ Well: Well specialists visually evaluate the overall condition and operability of the well system and/or individual components.

In each of these situations, remediation recommendations and cost estimates are also provided, if warranted.

Source: U.S. Inspect

Environmental Hazard Awareness

When you have a home inspection, insist on evaluation of environmental issues that may be present in or under the house, or on the property. Review the results with the seller and resolve it before the sale. The next step is to get a reputable environmental consulting firm to resolve any issues discovered during the inspection. The responsibility for costs and remediation should be stated in the contract.

> ***Hot Tip:***
>
> **Other Inspections to Note**
>
> **Structural engineer reports**: "If there is any doubt of the integrity of the structure (primarily due to foundational shift), it is important to hire a structural engineer to render an opinion (not only for the purchase decision, but ultimately as a baseline for resale)," says Smith of RE/MAX.
>
> **Stucco inspection**: Smith says if the property is made of synthetic stucco (EIFS), "I encourage the buyers I represent to get a stucco inspection which measures the moisture content behind the stucco to make sure no water is penetrating and evaluates any maintenance that needs to be performed."

John Brennan is the president of Brennan Environmental, Inc., an environmental consulting firm located in Summit, N.J. The company's growing roster of northeast clients covers a broad range of law firms, real estate brokerages, as well as insurance, engineering, and financial institutions. He offers tips on how to complete your environmental due diligence prior to closing on a house. He says, "These relatively simple guidelines will save you money and ease your mind through the home-buying process."

Outside the house

- Underground storage tanks: If the home is or ever was heated by oil from an underground storage tank, it should be tested for leakage or decommissioned if no longer in use. Soil samples from near the tank also should be tested for contamination. Cleanup from leaking underground storage tanks is very costly. Furthermore, make sure to get leak insurance for any active heating oil tanks on the property.
- Private wells: If the home has a private well, a water test for contamination and safety should be conducted, as it is harmful to drink contaminated water.
- Septic systems: Homes using a septic system or similar soil absorption system should be tested prior to purchase to avoid costly upgrade and replacement and to avoid unsanitary or dangerous site conditions from abandoned septic systems.

Inside the house

- Asbestos: Flooring, walls, ceiling tiles, boilers, and pipes should be tested for asbestos, which becomes problematic if asbestos-containing materials crumble, flake, or deteriorate through activities like cleaning, accidental damage, or renovation.
- Radon gas: A screening should be conducted, especially in the lower levels of the house. Radon is a cancer-causing radioactive gas that is undetectable by human senses.
- Lead: Interior and exterior painted surfaces should be tested for the presence of lead. This holds especially true

for any building that was built prior to 1978. Lead enters the dust and air inside a home when surfaces with lead-based paint deteriorate or are scraped, sanded, or heated in paint stripping procedures. Lead can also be present in water lines in which lead-based solder was used. If the home is built before 1978, you should receive an EPA-approved lead-based paint hazard pamphlet called Protect Your Family from Lead in Your Home (*www.epa.gov* or visit *www.hud.gov for* more on this issue).

- Mold: Wood, ceiling tiles, wallpaper, carpets, and insulation should be inspected for mold. Mold can cause respiratory illness and allergic reactions and is usually a sign of unacceptably high moisture levels in a home.

Hot Tip:

Two Other Toxic Hazards

If you know the seller has had certain problems with certain hazards in the past, it's a good idea to get the home tested for it. Two other toxic hazards to be aware of are:

1. Carbon monoxide: An invisible, odorless gas that can be found in stoves, gas fireplaces, wood burning, furnaces, space heaters, or automobiles.
2. Formaldehyde: A colorless, acrid gas found in building materials such as plywood, hardwood paneling, particleboard, paints, glues, foam insulation (homes built in the 70s), preservatives, some gas stoves, and kerosene space heaters.

The Inspection Report

Dan Osborn of Upstate Home Inspection Service says there is no standardized reporting system in the United States and there are many different types of reports: checklists, text, pre-printed paper reports, computer generated program reports, online reports, or any combination of these. He says, "There are as many reporting systems as there are inspectors. This is why it is important to know what kind of report you will be getting as well as how competent your inspector is."

He says, generally, the report is broken down to the different components of a house: exterior, interior, roof, bathrooms, kitchen, heating, electrical, and so on. He says each area is examined for different items. For example, an attic is looked at for water leaks, construction, insulation, ventilation, mold, and so on. If any of these items are not up to standards, then a concern will show on the report that that condition should be remedied. Some inspectors will add an approximate cost to that concern. Other inspectors will recommend that a qualified contractor review the concern and make recommendations.

Osborn says, "At this point it is up to the buyer as to whether he wants to do this before he buys the house or after. The job of the home inspector is to make sure he was *aware* of the condition."

Inspections Cover?

The National Association of Certified Home Inspectors shares with us the key areas that are typically covered in a home inspection, so you get an idea of what to expect:

- Roof: Gutters, downspouts, vents, flashings, skylights, chimney, other roof penetrations, roof covering, general structure of the roof from accessible panels, doors or stairs.
- Exterior: Doors, decks, stoops, steps, porches, railings, eaves, fascias, grading, walkways, balusters, spindles, balconies, surface drainage, and retaining walls likely to adversely affect the building.
- Basement, foundation, and crawlspace: Basement, foundation, crawlspace, visible structural components. Inspect for conditions of water penetration where deterioration is present. Report general indications of foundation movement,

such as cracks, brick cracks, out-of-square doorframes, sheetrock, or floor slopes.

- Heating: Inspect the heating system; describe the energy source and heating method using normal operating controls. Report as in need or repair, electric furnaces that do not operate. Report if the furnace is inaccessible.
- Cooling: Central cooling equipment using normal operating controls.
- Plumbing: Inspect the main water shut off valve and inspect water-heating system. Flush toilets. Run water in sinks, tubs and showers. Inspect fixtures, faucets, drain, waster and vent systems. Describe any visible fuel storage. Inspect drainage sump pumps (testing sumps with accessible floats). Inspect/describe water supply, drain, waste, main fuel shut-off.
- Attic, ventilation, insulation: Insulation in unfinished spaces, ventilation in the attic, mechanical ventilation systems, and report any general lack of insulation.
- Doors, windows, and interior: Open and close windows and doors. Inspect walls, ceilings, steps, stairways, railings, garage doors and door openers, electronic sensors and door locks. Check for windows in need of repair that are fogged or display other evidence of broken seals.
- Electrical: Service line, meter box, main disconnect, service amperage, panels, breakers, fuses, grounding, bonding, switches, receptacles, light fixtures, ground circuit interrupters, service entrance conductors (condition of their sheathing), ground fault circuit interrupters with GFCI tester, and service entrance cables. Report: Absence of smoke detectors, presence of solid conductor aluminum branch circuit wiring if readily visible, GFCI-tested receptacles where power isn't present, polarity is incorrect, not grounded, evidence of arcing or excessive heat, is not secured to the wall, cover is not in place or the ground fault

circuit interrupter devices are not properly installed or do not operate properly.

- Fireplace: Open/close the damper door if readily accessible and operable. Hearth extensions and other permanently installed components. Also, report those things in need pf repair, such as deficiencies in the lintel, hearth and material surrounding the fireplace, including clearance from combustible materials.

Source: NACHI

Chapter 10

To-Do Checklist: Before Closing

Now To Closing	Who Sets It Up
Buyer needs to obtain financing.	Buyer and loan officer.
Appraisal.	Loan officer.
Whole house inspection.	Realtor and buyer.
Repairs: Buyer requests after home inspection and, if any, lender-required repairs from the appraisal.	Seller.
Termite inspection.	Seller typically arranges it. (If it is a VA [Veterans Administration] loan, the seller is usually required to set it up.)
Well and septic inspection. You should not set up either one more than 30 days before closing. (If, in the last five years, the septic has not been pumped, get it taken care of.)	Buyer or seller.
Additional inspections (mold, roof, environmental, structural inspections, and so on).	Buyer.

Utilities.	Buyer and seller.
Survey.	The survey is usually not required by the lender except in the rare case that a title company is requiring it.)
Title search.	Title company.
Repairs approved by lender and buyer.	Lender, buyer, and seller.
Home insurance.	Buyer.
Go over closing costs, settlement statement, and paperwork.	Attorney, closing agent, or a title company, the buyer, and lender.
Bring cashier's check or certified funds to closing. (The closing officer will let you know what you need to pay at settlement.)	Buyer and seller. (Seller also needs to bring keys and garage door opener.)
Closing.	Closing is usually set up by the attorney/closing agent and buyer.

Take Care of Three Key Areas

After the contract is signed, there are three key areas that the sale depends on:

1. You need to obtain financing for the house (a.k.a. square away your loan): The sale depends on you getting approved for the loan to be able to afford your home. This is the reason sellers prefer that you have a pre-approval letter for a loan.

2. Lender's conditions: The lender has requirements before granting the loan. The lender will

want an appraisal (to assure the home's value), termite inspections (usually the seller sets this up, makes repairs or has damage treated, and show, proof it has been taken care of), title insurance (this protects against errors with the title), and title exam.

3. Inspections: The deal will be contingent on a whole house inspection, to get a physical examination of the property. For more on inspections, visit Chapter 9.

Who Will Handle Your Closing?

As soon as you have a deal, you need to find an attorney, closing agent, or title company to handle your closing. Closings typically take place 30, 45, or 60 days after the deal. If a buyer has all his or her ducks in a row, a closing can happen in a week in some areas or situations. The reason it doesn't tend to exceed 60 days is because it then becomes hard to lock in loan rates. If the rate goes up, the buyer may come across a situation in which he is no longer able to pay for the home.

When you have a fully executed contract, or even before, find a professional to handle your closing, such as a title company, real estate attorney, or escrow firm to take care of your closing (also commonly called settlement). Look at what services are offered by those in your area and select the one that best meets your needs.

Contact Info

Handy contacts to keep track of while buying a home.

Name:
Phone:
E-mail:
Address:

Name:
Phone:
E-mail:
Address:

Name:
Phone:
E-mail:
Address:

Name:
Phone:
E-mail:
Address:

Name:
Phone:
E-mail:
Address:

Name:
Phone:
E-mail:
Address:

Checklist Before Closing

- ☑ Reserve a rental truck or make arrangements with a moving company. It's always a good idea to set this up early.
- ☑ At least two weeks before you move, contact your utilities: electric, gas, telephone, refuse, cable, water company, and any other services.
- ☑ Take care of setting up utilities for your new home.
- ☑ Register your kids for school and ask for the school records to be transferred.
- ☑ Let your healthcare professionals know about your move (doctors, dentists, vet). If you are moving out of the area, ask for record transfers and referrals.
- ☑ Fill out an IRS change of address form.
- ☑ Fill out a change of address form for the post office.
- ☑ Make arrangements for moving your pets and plants.
- ☑ Start clearing out the fridge.

Preparations for moving out of state

- ☑ Set up travel arrangements with airlines, car rentals, buses, and hotels.
- ☑ Set up a checking account in your new location.
- ☑ Research relocation companies to help you move to a new area.
- ☑ Transfer memberships in clubs, organizations, and churches, and so on.

Chapter 11

Closing Day!
How to Avoid Common Closing Hiccups

Closing day is surprisingly the easiest part of the home-buying process. (It's getting everything in order before closing that is sometimes stressful.) Closing (also called settlement or escrow) is the transferring of ownership (or title) of the house. On closing day, you, the seller, the real estate agents involved, the title company (or real estate attorney), and representatives of the lender meet. In some areas, the closings are held in separate locations for the buyer and seller and in other areas, there is no formal closing where everyone meets. Instead the escrow agent takes care of the paperwork and then collects and distributes the funds.

During the closing, you will sign a huge stack of documents; your settlement agent, title company, or real estate attorney (who is taking care of your closing) will walk you through each document, what it means, and where to sign. You will pay the closing costs. Then, the keys to your new home are yours!

Hot Tip:

Review the paperwork before closing so you are familiar with the costs. Look at the HUD-1 settlement statement beforehand to see what you and the seller will be paying. Before closing, find out if you will receive your keys to move in that day, know how much is owed in down payment and closing costs, and find out the certified funds (such as cashier's check or official bank check) amount.

Prepare for a Smooth Closing

One common closing problem is that sometimes problems arise when loan documents arrive at closing and the terms and conditions are different than you were expecting. My number-one tip is to look at the loan documents well in advance of closing. It's always a good idea to keep in touch with the closing officer, attorney, or title company to make sure everything is moving along smoothly. The other ways you can prepare for a stress-free closing is by taking care of the following:

- ☑ Set a closing date.
- ☑ Select a closing agent, real estate attorney, or title company to handle your closing.
- ☑ Secure the loan.
- ☑ Secure a title service.
- ☑ Make sure the seller takes care of the termite inspection and has proof of repairs, if needed.
- ☑ Get homeowner's insurance.
- ☑ Get a homeowner's warranty.
- ☑ Attend a final walk-through.
- ☑ View the HUD-1 Settlement Statement before closing. It will show you the amount you need to bring to settlement in the form of certified funds (such as a certified check or official bank check).

When you attend the closing, you will be prepared to go over the documents, sign them, make your closing payment, and get the keys to your new home! (Make sure you get the garage keys, too!)

Behind the scenes, after everything is signed, fees are paid, the loan (or deed of trust) and your deed are recorded at the registry of deeds or county Recorder's Office. The funds are distributed. The legal transfer of your home typically takes one or two days after closing.

What Documents Will You Sign?

There are a few common documents you and the seller will be asked to sign at closing. The closing agent will typically walk you through each document and if you have any questions at all during the process, ask.

- Buyer typically signs: HUD-1 settlement statement, Truth in Lending disclosure statement, mortgage note, warranty deed, Real Estate Settlement Procedures Act (RESPA), loan application, "deed of trust" or mortgage, loan application, tax authorization, escrow analysis, and any other forms depending on local customs and laws (according to Ginnie Mae). Other forms: Homeowner's insurance and title insurance.
- Seller usually signs: HUD-1 settlement statement, grant or warranty deed, the bill of sale, escrow instruction, and any additional documents with the individual transaction.

Chapter 12

Sample Contracts: Contracts, Addendums, Disclosures, Disclaimers, and More!

Whenever there is a huge stack of contracts and paperwork in front of you, it's overwhelming. Most of the time, as you hear the mortgage person or attorney go over the legalities, and you nod and just pay attention to one key point: "Where do I sign?" This section give's you a general feel for what a sample contract, lead-based paint disclosure, disclaimer, disclosure, and more look like. When you sit down to look at the paperwork in your own home-buying transaction, you won't be blindly staring at it for the first time.

- Information about Brokerage Services.
- Intermediary Relationship Notice.
- Third Party Financing Condition Addendum.
- Seller's Disclosure Notice.
- Disclaimer/Disclosure.
- Lead-Based Paint Disclosure.

You may see forms similar to this in your own transaction. Depending on your personal experience, your forms may look different. This is to give you a general understanding for sample paperwork you may encounter.

Information About Brokerage Services

Approved by the Texas Real Estate Commission for Voluntary Use

Texas law requires all real estate licensees to give the following information about brokerage services to prospective buyers, tenants, sellers and landlords.

Information About Brokerage Services

Before working with a real estate broker, you should know that the duties of a broker depend on whom the broker represents. If you are a prospective seller or landlord (owner) or a prospective buyer or tenant (buyer), you should know that the broker who lists the property for sale or lease is the owner's agent. A broker who acts as a subagent represents the owner in cooperation with the listing broker. A broker who acts as a buyer's agent represents the buyer. A broker may act as an intermediary between the parties if the parties consent in writing. A broker can assist you in locating a property, preparing a contract or lease, or obtaining financing without representing you. A broker is obligated by law to treat you honestly.

IF THE BROKER REPRESENTS THE OWNER:
The broker becomes the owner's agent by entering into an agreement with the owner, usually through a written listing agreement, or by agreeing to act as a subagent by accepting an offer of subagency from the listing broker. A subagent may work in a different real estate office. A listing broker or subagent can assist the buyer but does not represent the buyer and must place the interests of the owner first. The buyer should not tell the owner's agent anything the buyer would not want the owner to know because an owner's agent must disclose to the owner any material information known to the agent.

IF THE BROKER REPRESENTS THE BUYER:
The broker becomes the buyer's agent by entering into an agreement to represent the buyer, usually through a written buyer representation agreement. A buyer's agent can assist the owner but does not represent the owner and must place the interests of the buyer first. The owner should not tell a buyer's agent anything the owner would not want the buyer to know because a buyer's agent must disclose to the buyer any material information known to the agent.

IF THE BROKER ACTS AS AN INTERMEDIARY:
A broker may act as an intermediary between the parties if the broker complies with The Texas Real Estate License Act. The broker must obtain the written consent of each party to the transaction to act as an intermediary. The written consent must state who will pay the broker and, in conspicuous bold or underlined print, set forth the broker's obligations as an intermediary. The broker is required to treat each party honestly and fairly and to comply with The Texas Real Estate License Act. A broker who acts as an intermediary in a transaction:

(1) shall treat all parties honestly;
(2) may not disclose that the owner will accept a price less than the asking price unless authorized in writing to do so by the owner;
(3) may not disclose that the buyer will pay a price greater than the price submitted in a written offer unless authorized in writing to do so by the buyer; and
(4) may not disclose any confidential information or any information that a party specifically instructs the broker in writing not to disclose unless authorized in writing to disclose the information or required to do so by The Texas Real Estate License Act or a court order or if the information materially relates to the condition of the property.

With the parties' consent, a broker acting as an intermediary between the parties may appoint a person who is licensed under The Texas Real Estate License Act and associated with the broker to communicate with and carry out instructions of one party and another person who is licensed under that Act and associated with the broker to communicate with and carry out instructions of the other party.

If you choose to have a broker represent you,
you should enter into a written agreement with the broker that clearly establishes the broker's obligations and your obligations. The agreement should state how and by whom the broker will be paid. You have the right to choose the type of representation, if any, you wish to receive. Your payment of a fee to a broker does not necessarily establish that the broker represents you. If you have any questions regarding the duties and responsibilities of the broker, you should resolve those questions before proceeding.

Real estate licensee asks that you acknowledge receipt of this information about brokerage services for the licensee's records.

Buyer, Seller, Landlord or Tenant   Date

Texas Real Estate Brokers and Salespersons are licensed and regulated by the Texas Real Estate Commission (TREC). If you have a question or complaint regarding a real estate licensee, you should contact TREC at P.O. Box 12188, Austin, Texas 78711-2188 or 512-465-3960.

01A   TREC No. OP-K

(TAR-2501) 1/1/96   Page 1 of 1

RE/MAX Professional Group 9234 FM 1960 West, Houston TX 77070
Phone: (832) 228-8268   Fax: Leslie Nichols   Forms For Pipe

Jntermediary Relationship Notice

TEXAS ASSOCIATION OF REALTORS®

INTERMEDIARY RELATIONSHIP NOTICE

To: ______________________________ **(Seller or Landlord)**

and ______________________________ **(Prospect)**

From: ______________________________ **(Broker's Firm)**

Re: ______________________________ **(Property)**

Date: ____________________

A. Under this notice, "owner" means the seller or landlord of the Property and "prospect" means the above-named prospective buyer or tenant for the Property.

B. Broker's firm represents the owner under a listing agreement and also represents the prospect under a buyer/tenant representation agreement.

C. In the written listing agreement and the written buyer/tenant representation agreement, both the owner and the prospect previously authorized Broker to act as an intermediary if a prospect who Broker represents desires to buy or lease a property that is listed by the Broker. When the prospect makes an offer to purchase or lease the Property, Broker will act in accordance with the authorizations granted in the listing agreement and in the buyer/tenant representation agreement.

D. Broker ☐ will ☐ will not appoint licensed associates to communicate with, carry out instructions of, and provide opinions and advice during negotiations to each party. If Broker makes such appointments, Broker appoints:

______________________________ to the owner; and

______________________________ to the prospect.

E. By acknowledging receipt of this notice, the undersigned parties reaffirm their consent for broker to act as an intermediary.

F. <u>Additional information</u>: *(Disclose material information related to Broker's relationship to the parties, such as personal relationships or prior or contemplated business relationships.)*

The undersigned acknowledge receipt of this notice

Seller or Landlord	Date	Prospect	Date
Seller or Landlord	Date	Prospect	Date

Third Party Financing Condition Addendum

02-13-06

PROMULGATED BY THE TEXAS REAL ESTATE COMMISSION (TREC)

THIRD PARTY FINANCING CONDITION ADDENDUM

TO CONTRACT CONCERNING THE PROPERTY AT

____

(Street Address and City)

Buyer shall apply promptly for all financing described below and make every reasonable effort to obtain approval for the financing (Financing Approval). Buyer shall furnish all information and documents required by lender for Financing Approval. Financing Approval will be deemed to have been obtained when (1) the terms of the loan(s) described below are available and (2) lender determines that Buyer has satisfied all of lender's financial requirements (those items relating to Buyer's assets, income and credit history). If Buyer cannot obtain Financing Approval, Buyer may give written notice to Seller within ______________ days after the effective date of this contract and this contract will terminate and the earnest money will be refunded to Buyer. **If Buyer does not give such notice within the time required, this contract will no longer be subject to Financing Approval. Time is of the essence for this paragraph and strict compliance with the time for performance is required.**

NOTE: Financing Approval does not include approval of lender's underwriting requirements for the Property, as specified in Paragraph 4.A.(1) of the contract.

Each note must be secured by vendor's and deed of trust liens.

CHECK APPLICABLE BOXES:

❑ A. CONVENTIONAL FINANCING:

❑ (1) A first mortgage loan in the principal amount of $ ______________________ (excluding any financed PMI premium), due in full in ______________ year(s), with interest not to exceed __________ % per annum for the first ______ year(s) of the loan with Loan Fees (loan origination, discount, buy-down, and commitment fees) not to exceed ______________ % of the loan.

❑ (2) A second mortgage loan in the principal amount of $ ____________________ (excluding any financed PMI premium), due in full in ________________ year(s), with interest not to exceed ______________ % per annum for the first ______ year(s) of the loan with Loan Fees (loan origination, discount, buy-down, and commitment fees) not to exceed ______________ % of the loan.

❑ B. TEXAS VETERANS HOUSING ASSISTANCE PROGRAM LOAN: A Texas Veterans Housing Assistance Program Loan of $ ________________ for a period of at least _______ years at the interest rate established by the Texas Veterans Land Board.

❑ C. FHA INSURED FINANCING: A Section __________________ FHA insured loan of not less than $ ______________________ (excluding any financed MIP), amortizable monthly for not less than _______ years, with interest not to exceed _________ % per annum for the first ______ year(s) of the loan with Loan Fees (loan origination, discount, buy-down, and commitment fees) not to exceed _____________ % of the loan. As required by HUD-FHA, if FHA valuation is unknown, *"It is expressly agreed that, notwithstanding any other provision of this contract, the purchaser (Buyer) shall not be obligated to complete the purchase of the Property described herein or to incur any penalty by forfeiture of earnest money deposits or otherwise unless the purchaser (Buyer) has been given in accordance with HUD/FHA or VA requirements a written statement issued by the Federal Housing Commissioner, Department of Veterans Affairs, or a Direct Endorsement Lender setting forth the appraised value of the Property of not less than $ __________________ . The purchaser (Buyer) shall have the privilege and option of proceeding with consummation of the contract without regard to the amount of the*

Initialed for identification by Buyer ____ ____ and Seller ____ ____

(TAR-1901) 2-13-06

TREC NO. 40-2

Page 1 of 2

RE/MAX Professional Group 9234 FM 1960 West, Houston TX 77070
Phone: (832) 228-8268 Fax: Leslie Nichols Forms For Pipe

____
(Address of Property)

appraised valuation. The appraised valuation is arrived at to determine the maximum mortgage the Department of Housing and Urban Development will insure. HUD does not warrant the value or the condition of the Property. The purchaser (Buyer) should satisfy himself/herself that the price and the condition of the Property are acceptable."

NOTE: HUD 92564-CN "For Your Protection: Get a Home Inspection" must be signed and dated by Buyer and attached to this Addendum.

❑ D. VA GUARANTEED FINANCING: A VA guaranteed loan of not less than $ ____________ (excluding any financed Funding Fee), amortizable monthly for not less than ________ years, with interest not to exceed ________ % per annum for the first ________ year(s) of the loan with Loan Fees (loan origination, discount, buy-down, and commitment fees) not to exceed ________ % of the loan.

VA NOTICE TO BUYER: *"It is expressly agreed that, notwithstanding any other provisions of this contract, the Buyer shall not incur any penalty by forfeiture of earnest money or otherwise or be obligated to complete the purchase of the Property described herein, if the contract purchase price or cost exceeds the reasonable value of the Property established by the Department of Veterans Affairs. The Buyer shall, however, have the privilege and option of proceeding with the consummation of this contract without regard to the amount of the reasonable value established by the Department of Veterans Affairs."*

If Buyer elects to complete the purchase at an amount in excess of the reasonable value established by VA, Buyer shall pay such excess amount in cash from a source which Buyer agrees to disclose to the VA and which Buyer represents will not be from borrowed funds except as approved by VA. If VA reasonable value of the Property is less than the Sales Price, Seller may reduce the Sales Price to an amount equal to the VA reasonable value and the sale will be closed at the lower Sales Price with proportionate adjustments to the down payment and the loan amount.

Buyer hereby authorizes any lender to furnish to the Seller or Buyer or their representatives information relating only to the status of Financing Approval of Buyer.

________________	________________
Buyer	Seller
________________	________________
Buyer	Seller

This form has been approved by the Texas Real Estate Commission for use with similarly approved or promulgated contract forms. Such approval relates to this form only. TREC forms are intended for use only by trained real estate licensees. No representation is made as to the legal validity or adequacy of any provision in any specific transactions. It is not intended for complex transactions. Texas Real Estate Commission, P.O. Box 12188, Austin, TX 78711-2188, 1-800-250-8732 or (512) 459-6544 (http://www.trec.state.tx.us) TREC No. 40-2. This form replaces TREC No. 40-1.

Seller's Disclosure Notice

TEXAS ASSOCIATION OF REALTORS®

SELLER'S DISCLOSURE NOTICE

Section 5.008, Property Code requires a seller of residential property of not more than one dwelling unit to deliver a Seller's Disclosure Notice to a buyer on or before the effective date of a contract. **This form complies with and contains additional disclosures which exceed the minimum disclosures required by the Code.**

CONCERNING THE PROPERTY AT ____

THIS NOTICE IS A DISCLOSURE OF SELLER'S KNOWLEDGE OF THE CONDITION OF THE PROPERTY AS OF THE DATE SIGNED BY SELLER AND IS NOT A SUBSTITUTE FOR ANY INSPECTIONS OR WARRANTIES THE BUYER MAY WISH TO OBTAIN. IT IS NOT A WARRANTY OF ANY KIND BY SELLER, SELLER'S AGENTS, OR ANY OTHER AGENT.

Seller ❒ is ❒ is not occupying the Property. If unoccupied (by Seller), how long since Seller has occupied the Property?
❒ ______________________________ or ❒ never occupied the Property

Section 1. The Property has the items marked below: (Mark Yes (Y), No (N), or Unknown (U).)

Note: This notice does not establish which items will or will not be conveyed.
The terms of a contract will determine which items will and will not be conveyed.

Item	Y	N	U	Item	Y	N	U	Item	Y	N	U
Cable TV Wiring				Gas Lines (Nat/LP)				Pool Heater			
Carbon Monoxide Det.				Hot Tub				Public Sewer System			
Ceiling Fans				Intercom System				Rain Gutters			
Cooktop				Microwave				Range/Stove			
Dishwasher				Outdoor Grill				Roof/Attic Vents			
Disposal				Oven				Sauna			
Exhaust Fans				Patio/Decking				Spa			
Fences				Plumbing System				Trash Compactor			
Fire Detection Equip.				Pool				TV Antenna			
French Drain				Pool Equipment				Washer/Dryer Hookup			
Gas Fixtures				Pool Maint. Accessories				Window Screens			

Item	Y	N	U	Additional Information
Central A/C				❒ electric ❒ gas number of units: ________
Wall/Window AC Units				number of units: ________
Attic Fan(s)				if yes, describe: ________
Evaporative Coolers				number of units: ________
Central Heat				❒ electric ❒ gas number of units: ________
Other Heat				if yes, describe: ________
Fireplace & Chimney				❒ woodburning _____ (no.) ❒ mock _____ (no.) other: ________
Carport				❒ attached ❒ not attached
Garage				❒ attached ❒ not attached
Garage Door Openers				number of units: ________ number of remotes: ________
Satellite Dish & Controls				❒ owned ❒ leased from ________
Security System				❒ owned ❒ leased from ________
Water Heater				❒ electric ❒ gas ❒ other: ________ number of units: ________
Water Softener				❒ owned ❒ leased from ________
Underground Lawn Sprinkler				❒ automatic ❒ manual areas covered: ________
Septic / On-Site Sewer Facility				if yes, attach Information About On-Site Sewer Facility (TAR-1407)

(TAR-1406) 4-26-04 Initialed by: Seller: _______ , _______ and Buyer: _______ , _______ Page 1 of 4

Concerning the Property at ____

Water supply provided by: ❒ city ❒ well ❒ MUD ❒ co-op ❒ unknown ❒ other: ____________________

Was the Property built before 1978? ❒ yes ❒ no ❒ unknown

(If yes, complete, sign, and attach TAR-1906 concerning lead-based paint hazards).

Roof Type: ____________________ Age: ____________________ (approximate)

Is there an overlay roof covering on the Property (shingles or roof covering placed over existing shingles or roof covering)?
❒ yes ❒ no ❒ unknown

Are you (Seller) aware of any of the items listed in this Section 1 that are not in working condition, that have defects, or are in need of repair? ❒ yes ❒ no If yes, describe (attach additional sheets if necessary): ____________________

____

____

____

Section 2. Are you (Seller) aware of any defects or malfunctions in any of the following?: (Mark Yes (Y) if you are aware and No (N) if you are not aware.)

Item	Y	N	Item	Y	N	Item	Y	N
Basement			Floors			Sidewalks		
Ceilings			Foundation / Slab(s)			Walls / Fences		
Doors			Interior Walls			Windows		
Driveways			Lighting Fixtures			Other Structural Components		
Electrical Systems			Plumbing Systems					
Exterior Walls			Roof					

If the answer to any of the items in Section 2 is yes, explain (attach additional sheets if necessary): ____________________

____

____

____

Section 3. Are you (Seller) aware of any of the following conditions: (Mark Yes (Y) if you are aware and No (N) if you are not aware.)

Condition	Y	N	Condition	Y	N
Aluminum Wiring			Previous Roof Repairs		
Asbestos Components			Other Structural Repairs		
Diseased Trees: ❒ oak wilt ❒ __________			Radon Gas		
Endangered Species/Habitat on Property			Settling		
Fault Lines			Soil Movement		
Hazardous or Toxic Waste			Subsurface Structure or Pits		
Improper Drainage			Underground Storage Tanks		
Intermittent or Weather Springs			Unplatted Easements		
Landfill			Unrecorded Easements		
Lead-Based Paint or Lead-Based Pt. Hazards			Urea-formaldehyde Insulation		
Encroachments onto the Property			Water Penetration		
Improvements encroaching on others' property			Wetlands on Property		
Located in 100-year Floodplain			Wood Rot		
Present Flood Insurance Coverage (If yes, attach TAR-1414)			Active infestation of termites or other wood-destroying insects (WDI)		
Previous Flooding into the Structures			Previous treatment for termites or WDI		
Previous Flooding onto the Property			Previous termite or WDI damage repaired		
Previous Fires			Termite or WDI damage needing repair		
Previous Foundation Repairs					

Concerning the Property at ____

If the answer to any of the items in Section 3 is yes, explain (attach additional sheets if necessary): ______________
____
____
____
____

Section 4. Are you (Seller) aware of any item, equipment, or system in or on the Property that is in need of repair, which has not been previously disclosed in this notice? ☐ yes ☐ no If yes, explain (attach additional sheets if necessary): ____
____
____
____
____

Section 5. Are you (Seller) aware of any of the following (Mark Yes (Y) if you are aware. Mark No (N) if you are not aware.)

Y	N	
☐	☐	Room additions, structural modifications, or other alterations or repairs made without necessary permits or not in compliance with building codes in effect at the time.
☐	☐	Homeowners' associations or maintenance fees or assessments. If yes, complete the following: Name of association: ______________________ Manager's name: ______________________ Phone: ______________________ Fees or assessments are: $ __________ per __________ and are: ☐ mandatory ☐ voluntary Any unpaid fees or assessment for the Property? ☐ yes ($ __________) ☐ no If the Property is in more than one association, provide information about the other associations below or attach information to this notice.
☐	☐	Any common area (facilities such as pools, tennis courts, walkways, or other) co-owned in undivided interest with others. If yes, complete the following: Any optional user fees for common facilities charged? ☐ yes ☐ no If yes, describe: ______________________
☐	☐	Any notices of violations of deed restrictions or governmental ordinances affecting the condition or use of the Property.
☐	☐	Any lawsuits or other legal proceedings directly or indirectly affecting the Property.
☐	☐	Any death on the Property except for those deaths caused by: natural causes, suicide, or accident unrelated to the condition of the Property.
☐	☐	Any condition on the Property which materially affects the health or safety of an individual.
☐	☐	Any repairs or treatments, other than routine maintenance, made to the Property to remediate environmental hazards such as asbestos, radon, lead-based paint, urea-formaldehyde, or mold. If yes, attach any certificates or other documentation identifying the extent of the remediation (for example, certificate of mold remediation or other remediation).

If the answer to any of the items in Section 5 is yes, explain (attach additional sheets if necessary): ______________
____
____
____
____

Section 6. Do you (Seller) have a survey of the Property available for review?: ☐ yes ☐ no If yes, a copy of the survey ☐ is ☐ is not attached.

(TAR-1406) 4-26-04 Initialed by: Seller: _______ , _______ and Buyer: _______ , _______ Page 3 of 4

Concerning the Property at ____

Section 7. Within the last 4 years, have you (Seller) received any written inspection reports from persons who regularly provide inspections and who are either licensed as inspectors or otherwise permitted by law to perform inspections? ❒ yes ❒ no If yes, attach copies and complete the following:

Inspection Date	Type	Name of Inspector	No. of Pages

Note: A buyer should not rely on the above-cited reports as a reflection of the current condition of the Property. A buyer should obtain inspections from inspectors chosen by the buyer.

Section 8. Check any tax exemption(s) which you (Seller) currently claim for the Property:
❒ Homestead ❒ Senior Citizen ❒ Disabled ❒ Disabled Veteran ❒ Agricultural ❒ Wildlife Management
❒ Other: ______________________________ ❒ Unknown

Section 9. Have you (Seller) ever received proceeds for a claim for damage to the Property (for example, an insurance claim or a settlement or award in a legal proceeding) and not used the proceeds to make the repairs for which the claim was made? ❒ yes ❒ no If yes, explain: ______________________________

Seller acknowledges that the statements in this notice are true to the best of Seller's belief and that no person, including the broker(s), has instructed or influenced Seller to provide inaccurate information or to omit any material information.

Signature of Seller	Date	Signature of Seller	Date
Printed name:		Printed name:	

NOTICES TO BUYER:

The Texas Department of Public Safety maintains a database that the public may search, at no cost, to determine if registered sex offenders are located in certain zip code areas. To search the database, visit www.txdps.state.tx.us. For information concerning past criminal activity in certain areas or neighborhoods, contact the local police department.

If you are basing your offers on square footage, measurements, or boundaries, you should have those items independently measured to verify any reported information.

This Seller's Disclosure Notice was completed by Seller as of the date signed. The brokers have relied on this notice as true and correct and have no reason to believe it to be false or inaccurate. YOU ARE ENCOURAGED TO HAVE AN INSPECTOR OF YOUR CHOICE INSPECT THE PROPERTY.

The undersigned Buyer acknowledges receipt of the foregoing notice.

Signature of Buyer	Date	Signature of Buyer	Date
Printed name:		Printed name:	

Disclaimer/Disclosure

RESIDENTIAL PROPERTY DISCLOSURE AND DISCLAIMER STATEMENT

INSTRUCTIONS TO THE SELLER

Please complete the following form. Do not leave any spaces blank. If the question clearly does not apply to the property write "NA". If the answer to any items requires explanation, explain on attached sheets, if necessary.

NOTICE TO THE BUYER

THE FOLLOWING DISCLOSURES ARE MADE BY THE SELLER(S), CONCERNING THE CONDITION OF THE PROPERTY LOCATED AT 123 Any Street, Anytown, Alabama, 38383. ("THE PROPERTY"), OR AS LEGALLY DESCRIBED ON ATTACHED EXHIBIT A.

DISCLOSURES CONTAINED IN THIS FORM ARE PROVIDED BY THE SELLER ON THE BASIS OF SELLER'S ACTUAL KNOWLEDGE OF THE PROPERTY AT THE TIME THIS DISCLOSURE FORM IS COMPLETED BY THE SELLER. THE FOLLOWING ARE DISCLOSURES MADE BY THE SELLER AND ARE NOT THE REPRESENTATIONS OF ANY REAL ESTATE LICENSEE OR OTHER PARTY. THIS INFORMATION IS FOR DISCLOSURE ONLY AND IS NOT INTENDED TO BE A PART OF ANY WRITTEN AGREEMENT BETWEEN THE BUYER AND THE SELLER.

FOR A MORE COMPREHENSIVE EXAMINATION OF THE SPECIFIC CONDITION OF THIS PROPERTY YOU ARE ADVISED TO OBTAIN AND PAY FOR THE SERVICES OF A QUALIFIED SPECIALIST TO INSPECT THE PROPERTY ON YOUR BEHALF, FOR EXAMPLE, ARCHITECTS, ENGINEERS, LAND SURVEYORS, PLUMBERS, ELECTRICIANS, ROOFERS, BUILDING INSPECTORS, OR PEST AND DRY ROT INSPECTORS. THE PROSPECTIVE BUYER AND THE OWNER MAY WISH TO OBTAIN PROFESSIONAL ADVICE OR INSPECTIONS OF THE PROPERTY AND TO PROVIDE FOR APPROPRIATE PROVISIONS IN A CONTRACT BETWEEN THEM WITH RESPECT TO ANY ADVICE, INSPECTION, DEFECTS OR WARRANTIES.

Sellers, John Smith and Jane Smith, are currently occupying the property.
Seller has owned the property for 5 years.

I. SELLER'S DISCLOSURES. If explanation is needed, use attached sheet if necessary. Approximations should be labeled as such.

1. TITLE	YES	NO	UNKNOWN
A. Do you have legal authority to sell the property?	X		
B. Is title to the property subject to any of the following?			
(1) First right of refusal		X	
If yes, explain:			
(2) Option		X	
If yes, explain:			
(3) Lease or Rental Agreement		X	
If yes, explain:			
(4) Life Estate		X	
If yes, explain:			
C. Are there any encroachments, boundary disputes, or boundary agreements?		X	
If yes, explain:			
D. Are there any rights of way, easements, or access limitations that may affect the owner's use of the property?		X	
If yes, explain:			
E. Are there any written agreements for joint maintenance of an easement or right of way?		X	
If yes, explain:			
F. Is there any study, survey project, or notice that would adversely affect the property?		X	
If yes, explain:			
G. Are there any pending or existing assessments against the property?		X	
If yes, explain:			
H. Are there any zoning violations, nonconforming uses, or any unusual restrictions on the subject property that would affect future construction or remodeling?		X	
If yes, explain:			
I. Is there a boundary survey for the property? If yes, attach survey.		X	
J. Are the property's boundaries marked?	X		

1. TITLE	YES	NO	UNKNOWN
If yes, explain: Boundaries are fenced.			
K. Are there fences on the property?	X		
If yes, were the fences put up by the property owner?	X		
L. Are any trees or other flora on the property diseased, dead or damaged?			X
If yes, explain:			
M. Are there any covenants, conditions, or restrictions which affect the property?		X	
If yes, explain:			
N. Is the property accessed by public or private road?	(PUBLIC)	PRIVATE	UNKNOWN
If private, what yearly upkeep amount is paid by the property owner?			
If private, explain road upkeep in detail:			

2. WATER				
A. Household Water				
(1) The source of the water is:	(Public)	Community	Private	Shared
(2) Water source information:		YES	NO	UNKNOWN
a. Are there any written agreements for shared water source?			X	
If yes, explain:				
b. Is there an easement (recorded or unrecorded) for access to and/or maintenance of the water source?			X	
If yes, explain:				
c. Are any known problems or repairs needed?			X	
If yes, explain:				
d. Does the source provide an adequate year round supply of potable water?		X		
e. Are there any water treatment systems (softener, purifier, etc.) for the property?			X	
If yes, explain, and state if the system(s) is/are leased or owned:				
B. Irrigation				
(1) Are there any water rights for the property?			X	
If yes, explain:				
(2) If they exist, to your knowledge, have the water rights been used during the last five-year period?				
If yes, explain:				
(3) If so, is the certificate available?				
Explain:				
C. Outdoor Sprinkler System				
(1) Is there an outdoor sprinkler system for the property?			X	
(2) Are there any defects in the outdoor sprinkler system?			X	
If yes, explain:				

3. SEWER/SEPTIC SYSTEM			
A. The property is served by (circle one):	(Public Sewer Main)	Septic Tank System	Other Disposal System
If other, describe:			
B. If the property is served by a public or community sewer main, is the house connected to the main?	(Yes)	No	Unknown
If no, explain:			
C. Is the property currently subject to a sewer capacity charge?	Yes	(No)	Unknown
If yes, explain:			
D. If the property is connected to a septic system complete the following items (if no septic system, ignore these items):			
(1) Was a permit issued for its construction, and was it approved by the city or county following its construction?	Yes	No	Unknown
(2) On what date was it last pumped:			
(3) Are there any defects in the operation of the septic system?	Yes	No	Unknown
If yes, explain:			
(4) On what date was it last inspected:			
By whom:			
(5) How many bedrooms was the system approved for?			
(6) Are you aware of any changes or repairs to the septic system?	Yes	No	Unknown
If yes, explain:			

(7) Is the septic system, including drainage field, located entirely within the property's boundaries?	Yes	No	Unknown
If no, explain:			
E. Do all plumbing fixtures, including laundry drain, go to the septic/sewer system?	Yes	No	Unknown
If no, explain:			

4. STRUCTURAL

A. How old is the current roof? 10 years. (If unknown, mark Unknown.)			Unknown
Roof is constructed of: ☐ Asphalt Shingle, ☐ Wood Shingle, ☐ Slate, ☐ Metal, ☐ Tile, ☒ Asbestos, ☐ Unknown, ☐ Other:			
B. Has the roof leaked during your ownership?	Yes	No	Unknown
If yes, has it been repaired?	Yes	No	
Explain any roof repairs of which you are aware:			
C. Has the house undergone any conversions, additions, or remodeling?	Yes	No	Unknown
1. If yes, were all building permits obtained?	Yes	No	Unknown
2. If yes, were all final inspections obtained?	Yes	No	Unknown
Explain any conversions/additions/remodeling:			

D. Do you know the age of the house?	Yes	No
If yes, give year of original construction (if approximation, indicate such):		
E. Are you aware of:		
(1) Any movement, shifting, deterioration or other problems with walls, foundation, crawl space or slab?	Yes	No
(2) Any cracks or flaws in the walls, ceilings, foundations, concrete slab, crawl space, basement, floors or garage?	Yes	No
(3) Any water leakage or dampness in the crawl space or basement?	Yes	No
(4) Any dry rot on the property?	Yes	No
(5) Any repairs or other attempts to control the cause or effect of any problem described above?	Yes	No
Explain any 'Yes' answer(s) to 1-5 above. When describing repairs or control efforts, describe the location, extent, date, and name of person/company who did the work. Attach any reports and/or other documentation.		

F. If you know of any defect(s) regarding the following items, mark the defective item with a check:

1. Foundation ☐	6. Fire Alarm ☐	11. Slab Floors ☐	16. Sidewalks ☐	21. Balconies ☐
2. Deck ☐	7. Doors ☐	12. Driveways ☐	17. Outbuildings ☐	22. Wood Stoves ☐
3. Exterior walls ☐	8. Door locks ☐	13. Attic Stairs ☐	18. Fireplaces ☐	
4. Chimneys ☐	9. Patio ☐	14. Windows ☐	19. Garage Floors ☐	
5. Interior walls ☐	10. Ceilings ☐	15. Window locks ☐	20. Walkways ☐	

If you checked any of the above items, explain the defect(s):

G. In the last 4 years, was a pest, dry rot, structural or "whole house" inspection done?	Yes	No	Unknown
If yes, which test(s), when, and by whom was the inspection done? (Attach documentation)			
H. Has the property had a problem with pest control, infestations, or vermin?	Yes	No	Unknown
If yes, explain:			
I. Are you aware of:			
(1) Any termites, wood destroying insects or pests on or affecting the property?	Yes	No	
(2) Property damage by termites, wood destroying insects or pests?	Yes	No	
If yes, describe:			
(3) Any termite/pest control treatments on the property in the last 4 years?	Yes	No	
If yes, list company and where treated:			
(4) Current warranty or other coverage by a licensed pest control company on the property?	Yes	No	

If yes, explain warranty and attach documentation:		
J. Have you made a homeowner's insurance claim(s) regarding the property in the last 4 years?	Yes	No
If yes, explain when and why:		

5. SYSTEMS AND FIXTURES

If the following systems or fixtures are included with the transfer, do they have any existing defects:					YES	NO	UNKNOWN
A. Electrical system, including wiring, all switches, all outlets, and service						X	
If yes, explain:							
What type of wiring comprises the electrical system?				Copper		Aluminum	Unknown
B. Plumbing system, including pipes, faucets, fixtures, and toilets						X	
If yes, explain:							
C. Hot water heater (mark one):	Electric	Natural Gas	Other:	Age: 5 years		X	
If yes, explain:							
D. Oven/stove:	Electric	Natural Gas	Other:	Age: 3 years		X	
If yes, explain:							
E. List ANY OTHER APPLIANCES TO REMAIN, attach separate sheet if necessary.							
1. Refrigerator	Age: 25 years				YES	NO	UNKNOWN
If yes, explain: It leaks, smokes, and rattles.							
2.	Age: ____ years						
If yes, explain:							
3.	Age: ____ years						
If yes, explain:							

F. Cooling and Heating systems						
Air Conditioning (mark one):	Central Electric	Central Gas	Heat Pump	Window Unit(s) ____ # included in sale		
	Other (describe):					
Air Conditioning (continued)	Age of cooling system: 10 years.		Zoned cooling? [Yes] [No]			
Air Conditioning defects?	No	Unknown	Yes, explain:			
Heating system (mark one):	Electric	Natural Gas	Fuel Oil	Heat Pump	Propane	Other:
	Age of heating system: 9 years.		Zoned heating? [Yes] [No]			
Heating system defects?	No	Unknown	Yes, explain:			
Last date of servicing:	Heating: 11/12/03	Cooling: 11/12/03	By whom: Anytown Alabama Servicers Co.			
Are there rooms without heating/air conditioning vents?	Yes	No				
If yes, which rooms:						

G. Security system (Circle One):	Owned	Leased	None	Any defects?:	Yes	No	Unknown
Describe security system:							
If defects are indicated, explain:							
H. Other:				Any defects?	Yes	No	Unknown
If defects are indicated, explain:							

6. COMMON INTEREST

A. Is there a Home Owners' Association?			Yes	No	Unknown
If yes, what is the name of the association?					
B. Are there regular periodic assessments:			Yes	No	Unknown
If yes, give amount per:	Month: $	Year: $	Other: $		
If other, explain:					
C. Are there any pending special assessments?			Yes	No	Unknown
D. Are there any shared "common areas" or any joint maintenance agreements (facilities such as walls, fences, landscaping, pools, tennis courts, walkways, or other areas co-owned in undivided interest with others)?			Yes	No	Unknown

If any such areas exist, explain:

7. APPLIANCES, HEATING, PLUMBING, ELECTRICAL and OTHER MECHANICAL SYSTEMS

Instructions: Mark **INCL** if the item is included in the sale. If item is included in sale, mark **Yes** or **No** to indicate whether item is in working order. Indicate the item's approximate age (in years) in the 'age' space, if provided-- if age is unknown, mark '?' in space.

ITEM	INCL	Yes	No	ITEM	INCL	Yes	No
Attic Fan				Lawn Sprinkler Auto-timer			
Air Conditioner (central) age:10yrs	X	X		Lawn Sprinkler Backflow Valve			
Air Conditioner (wall/window) age:				Microwave Oven age:			
Air Cleaner/Purifier age:				Plumbing			
Ceiling Fan(s), # included ____				Pool age:			
Clothes Washer age:				Pool Equipment/ mechanisms age:			
Convection Oven age:				Range/Oven age: 3yrs	X	X	
Dishwasher age:				Range Timer			
Door Bells	X	X		Range Vent-hood			
Drain Tile System				Refrigerator age:25yrs	X		X
Dryer age:				Security System			
Exhaust Fans (bathroom)	X	X		Smoke Detectors (battery)	X	X	
Fireplace				Smoke Detectors (hardwired)			
Fireplace Mechanisms				Solar Collectors			
Furnace age:				Sump Pump			
Furnace Mechanisms				Toilet Mechanisms	X	X	
Freezer age:				TV Antenna/ receiver/ dish			
Garbage Compactor				TV Cable wiring			
Garbage Disposal				Water Heater age: 5yrs	X	X	
Garage Door Opener (GDO)				Window Treatments			
GDO Auto-reverse Safety Mechanism				Whirlpool/Hot-tub age:			
GDO Remote Opener(s), # included: ____				Wood Burning Stove			
Gas Grill				Yard Lights			
Gas Logs				Other:			
Heating System (central) age: 9yrs	X	X		Other:			
Heating System (supplemental) age:				Other:			
Humidifier age:				Other:			
Incinerator				Other:			
Intercom				Other:			
Lawn Sprinkler System				Other:			

Explanations: If any item above is NOT in working order, list the item and explain the defect in the space below.

8. GENERAL	YES	NO	UNKNOWN
A. Is there any settling, soil, standing water, or drainage problems on the property?		X	
If yes, explain:			
B. Does the property contain fill material?		X	
C. Is there any material damage to the property or any of the structure from fire, wind, floods, beach movements, earthquake, expansive soils, or landslides?		X	
If yes, explain:			
D. Is the property in a designated flood plain?	X		
E. Are there any substances, materials, or products that may be an environmental hazard such as, but not limited to, asbestos, formaldehyde, radon gas, lead-based paint, fuel or chemical storage tanks and contaminated soil or water on the subject property?	X		
If yes, explain: the roof is an asbestos roof			
F. Are there any tanks or underground storage tanks (e.g., chemical, fuel, etc.) on the property?		X	
If yes, explain, and give approx. position (attach map):			
G. Has the property ever been used as an illegal drug-manufacturing site?		X	

If yes, explain:		
H. If the property contains a wood-burning stove or fireplace, when was/were the chimney(ies) last cleaned?		
Detail date(s) and chimney(ies), or mark Unknown:		
I. Are you aware of any of the following regarding the property?		
Existing or threatened legal action ☐	Violation of any law or regulation ☐	General stains or pet stains to carpet or floor ☐
Transferable warranties ☐	Any locks without keys ☐	Unrecorded interests affecting the property ☐
Fire Damage at any time ☐	Appraiser or Mechanic's Lien ☐	Landfills or underground problems ☐
If any of the above are marked, explain:		
J. If any tests to detect **radon gas** have been done on the property, provide documentation. If radon gas has been detected on the property, explain when, where, by whom, and all other details:		

9. FULL DISCLOSURE BY SELLERS

	Yes	No
A. Other conditions or defects:		
Does the Seller know of any other material defects affecting this property or its value that a prospective buyer should know about?		X
If yes, explain:		

B. Verification:

The foregoing answers and attached explanations (if any) are complete and correct to the best of my/our knowledge and I/we have received a copy hereof. I/we authorize all of my/our real estate licensees, if any, to deliver a copy of this disclosure statement to other real estate licensees and all prospective buyers of the property.

11-13-05	John Smith	Jane Smith
Date	Seller	Seller

II. BUYER'S ACKNOWLEDGMENT

A. As buyer(s), I/we acknowledge the duty to pay diligent attention to any material defects which are known to me/us or can be known to me/us by utilizing diligent attention and observation.

B. Each buyer acknowledges and understands that the disclosures set forth in this statement and in any amendments to this statement are made only by the seller.

C. Buyer (which term includes all persons signing the buyer's acknowledgement portion of this disclosure statement below) hereby acknowledges receipt of a copy of this disclosure statement (including attachments, if any) bearing seller's signature.

DISCLOSURES CONTAINED IN THIS FORM ARE PROVIDED BY THE SELLER ON THE BASIS OF SELLER'S ACTUAL KNOWLEDGE OF THE PROPERTY AT THE TIME OF DISCLOSURE.

BUYER HEREBY ACKNOWLEDGES RECEIPT OF A COPY OF THIS REAL PROPERTY TRANSFER DISCLOSURE STATEMENT AND ACKNOWLEDGES THAT THE DISCLOSURES MADE HEREIN ARE THOSE OF THE SELLER ONLY, AND NOT OF ANY REAL ESTATE LICENSEE OR OTHER PARTY.

11-13-05	Tom Brown	
DATE	BUYER	BUYER

Lead–Based Paint Disclosure

Lead-Based Paint Disclosure (Sales)

123 Any Street Anytown Alabama 38383
Street Address City State Zip

WARNING! LEAD FROM PAINT, DUST, AND SOIL CAN BE DANGEROUS IF NOT MANAGED PROPERLY

Disclosure of Information on Lead-Based Paint and/or Lead-Based Paint Hazards

Lead Warning Statement

Every purchaser of any interest in residential real property on which a residential dwelling was built prior to 1978 is notified that such property may present exposure to lead from lead-based paint that may place young children at risk of developing lead poisoning. Lead poisoning in young children may produce permanent neurological damage, including learning disabilities, reduced intelligence quotient, behavioral problems, and impaired memory. Lead poisoning also poses a particular risk to pregnant women. The Seller of any interest in residential real property is required to provide the buyer with any information on lead-based paint hazards from risk assessments or inspections in the Seller's possession and notify the buyer of any known lead-based paint hazards. A risk assessment or inspection for possible lead-based paint hazards is recommended prior to purchase.

Seller's Disclosure

(a) Presence of lead-based paint and/or lead-based paint hazards (check (i) or (ii) below):

(i) ______ Known lead-based paint and/or lead-based paint hazards are present in the housing (explain).

____

(ii) __X__ Seller has no knowledge of lead-based paint and/or lead-based paint hazards in the housing.

(b) Records and reports available to the seller (check (i) or (ii) below):

(i) ______ Seller has provided the purchaser with all available records and reports pertaining to lead-based paint and/or lead-based paint hazards in the housing (list documents below).

____

(ii) __X__ Seller has no reports or records pertaining to lead-based paint and/or lead-based paint hazards in the housing.

Purchaser's Acknowledgment (initial)

(c) __TB__ Purchaser has received copies of all information listed above.

(d) __TB__ Purchaser has received the pamphlet *Protect Your Family from Lead in Your Home.*

(e) Purchaser has (check (i) or (ii) below):

(i) __X__ received a 10-day opportunity (or mutually agreed upon period) to conduct a risk assessment or inspection for the presence of lead-based paint and/or lead-based paint hazards; or

(ii) _____ waived the opportunity to conduct a risk assessment or inspection for the presence of lead-based paint and/or lead-based paint hazards.

Agent's Acknowledgment (initial)

(f) ________ Agent has informed the seller of the seller' obligations under 42 U.S.C. 4852(d) and is aware of his/her responsibility to ensure compliance.

Seller Initials: __JS__ __JS__ **Buyer Initials:** __TB__ ______ **Agent Initials:** ______ ______

Certification of Accuracy

The following parties have reviewed the information above and certify, to the best of their knowledge, that the information they have provided is true and accurate. **Penalties for failure to comply with Federal Lead-Based Paint Disclosure Laws include treble (3 times) damages, attorney fees, costs, and a penalty up to $10,000 for each violation.**

John Smith	11/13/05	Tom Brown	11/13/05
Seller	Date	Buyer	Date
Jane Smith	11/13/05		
Seller	Date	Buyer	Date
Agent	Date	Agent	Date

Chapter 13

Your Legal Rights: Home-Buying and Loan Borrower Rights to Protect You

What are your rights as a homebuyer and as a loan borrower?

Often, that is the part overlooked in the pursuit of a perfect home. Jeffrey P. Zane, Esquire and president of the Attorney's Real Estate Council of Palm Beach County, Inc., in Palm Beach Gardens, Florida, advised about common mistakes home buyers experience in purchasing a home, how to protect yourself in a sales contract, what to be prepared for when you go to closing, and more. (For more information about your mortgage borrower's rights, check with the U.S. Department of Housing and Urban Development.)

Piper: What are the most common mistakes home buyers experience in purchasing a home?

Jeffrey: [Home buyers] don't retain a real estate attorney to guide them through the process, they don't obtain a professional inspector for the property, and they don't try to obtain various loan possibilities for this purchase.

Piper: What should buyers be prepared for when going to sign the closing paperwork?

Jeffrey: They should have a real estate attorney with them to explain the documents. The expenditure of moneys is a relatively modest fee that protects them from their lack of experience in this area. That lack of experience can easily cost them a great deal of money.

Piper: What kinds of protection are there if you buy from a "for sale by owner" versus the regular route? Or is there even a difference?

Jeffrey: If you have a real estate attorney on your side during the process there will be no difference.

Piper: What recourse do buyers have if they get into the house and it's not as described—defects are found later after you've already closed (and you did a home inspection that didn't reveal either)? What are your options in this situation?

Jeffrey: The normal procedure is to make a final walk-through prior to closing. At the time of closing you should have the seller's possessions out of the property so there will be no surprises after closing.

Piper: What common clauses should be in the contract to protect your rights and interests?

Jeffrey: The easiest method to follow is to use a FAR [Florida Association of Realtors/you'r state's association of realtors]/BAR contract form, which has been designed to be fair to both the seller and the buyer. You should also have your real estate attorney review the contract prior to executing it.

Piper: If before closing you decide you no longer want the house, what are your options?

Jeffrey: They are limited by the terms of the contract. However, absent a defined problem reflected in the inspection report or the buyer's failure to qualify for financing in a deal with a financing contingency, you cannot terminate the contract without the consent of the seller. (To see more information on this topic, visit Chapter 7, page 121.)

Piper: Whose name should be on the deed of sale and what entanglements are significant others (roommate, sibling, spouse)? Or is it better to purchase in your own name? How does it affect inheritance issues besides, children?

Jeffrey: Besides married couples purchasing a property, no one should purchase a property jointly without there being a written agreement between the parties. You need an attorney to handle this matter.

Piper: If you die, who takes over the payments? Is there a clause that should be included to provide for the surviving spouse? If you don't have anyone, who does the house go to?

Jeffrey: Upon the owner's death, the property would go to any joint owner that has rights of survivorship. Absent that joint owner, it would go by the laws of homestead, or intestacy, or by the structure of a will or trust. The payments of the loan would depend upon the specific circumstances.

Mortgage Borrower's Rights

The U.S. Department of Housing and Urban Development has a list of certain rights you have and should be aware of before you agree to any loan agreement.

- You have the right to shop for the best loan for you and compare the charges of different mortgage brokers and lenders.
- You have the right to be informed about the total cost of your loan including the interest rate, points, and other fees.
- You have the right to ask for a Good Faith Estimate of all loan and settlement charges before you agree to the loan and pay any fees.
- You have the right to know what fees are not refundable if you decide to cancel the loan agreement.
- You have the right to ask your mortgage broker to explain exactly what the mortgage broker will do for you.
- You have the right to know how much the mortgage broker is getting paid by you and the lender for your loan.
- You have the right to ask questions about charges and loan terms that you do not understand.
- You have the right to a credit decision that is not based on your race, color, religion, national origin, sex, marital status, age, or whether any income is from public assistance.
- You have the right to know the reason if your loan was turned down.
- You have the right to ask for the HUD settlement costs booklet "Buying Your Home."

Source: *HUD.gov*

For "Buying Your Home" and other helpful information about RESPA, visit *www.hud.gov.* For other questions, call (800) 569-4287.

Chapter 14

Tax Perks and Breaks of Home Ownership: Putting Money Back in Your Pocket

We always hear there are tax perks and breaks of home ownership, so, for advice in this area, Sandy Botkin CPA, Esq., a former IRS attorney and trainer of IRS attorneys is here to help. He is the principal lecturer for the Tax Reduction Institute of Germantown, Maryland, and author of *Real Estate Tax Secrets of the Rich* (McGraw-Hill) and *Lower Your Taxes: BIG TIME* (McGraw-Hill).

Piper: What really are the benefits of home ownership?

Botkin: Homeownership is one of the greatest tax breaks given by Congress. Not only can you deduct interest on acquisition loans up to $1,000,000 of debt, home equity interest on debt up to $100,000, and also property taxes, you might even be able to deduct interest on any amount of debt, without any limit, with the Botkin Interest Maneuver, which is found in the frequently asked questions of my book, *Real Estate Tax Strategies of the Rich*.

I should note that the deduction on home acquision interest is available for both your principal residence and one second home. Thus, if you have several residences besides your principal home, pick the second home that gives the greatest deductions. This can be done yearly.

When you sell your home, you don't pay tax on up to $250,000 of gain if you are single or up to $500,000 of gain if you are married filing jointly. To meet this exclusion, you have to own and occupy the home for two out of the last five years.

Piper: Home ownership tax deductions: What can and can't you deduct? How do you figure out how much you can deduct and what tax paperwork you need to file? Which home expenses can you not deduct?

Botkin: What you can deduct: Interest on acquision debt of up to $1,000,000 of debt and interest on home equity debt of up to $100,000. You can deduct property taxes too. If you are eligible for a home office deduction, you can deduct part of the interest and taxes on your schedule C as a business expense, in addition to deducting part of the repairs, maintenance, utilities, depreciation, and so forth.

If you sell your home at a loss, you *cannot* take a loss on your home if it isn't used for business, such as a rental property. Losses on principal residences and second homes aren't deductible. Also, if you are subject to the alternative minimum tax, you won't be able to deduct property taxes and interest on home equity debit. This is an example of a congressional "gotcha."

I should note that although sale of homes at a loss is not deductible, you may take a deduction for the basis in your home and for the loss of any items in the home if it is destroyed by a casualty that isn't reimbursed by insurance. A casualty is a sudden, unexpected event. Thus, if your home was destroyed by the flood in hurricane Katrina, you may take a casualty loss on your home, although your loss must exceed 10 percent of your adjusted gross income plus $100. Thus, there is a threshold amount by which your loss must exceed in order to be deductible. Other examples of casualties would be damage from earthquake, tornado, terrorist attack, and so on.

Losses incurred in areas declared to be a Presidential Disaster (such as arising from Katrina), would be deductible either in the year of the disaster or can be taken in the previous year.

Congressional gotcha: The problem with claiming casualty losses, such as what happened to hurricane Katrina victims, is that they probably lost all support for their basis, which would give almost no deduction. Perhaps checking the land records posted with the county may enable these folks to get some benefit, assuming that the land records didn't float away. This is why all support for basis, such as closing statements and settlement papers, should be kept in a fireproof and water proof safe or safety deposit box.

You can also deduct all points paid to get a loan *if* the loan is for the acquisition or improvement of your principal residence. Thus, if you pay $2,000 to get a loan on acquiring your principal residence, it is fully deductible as interest.

Note: Points paid on loans that don't involve the acquistion or improvement of your principal residence get amortized over the life of the loan. Thus, if you incur points to refinance your loan or to acquire investment property, or for a second home, these points must be written off over the life of the loan.

MONEY SAVER:

What happens if you have non-deductible points and you refinance the loan or sell the property?

You get to deduct all of the points that you previously didn't deduct. Most people miss this because they may have paid these non-deductible points many years ago. It is vital to check your original settlement statement or prior lending statement to see if there were any points that were incurred but not deducted.

Piper: How does home improvement affects your taxes?

Botkin: The key is understanding basis. Basis is generally what you paid for your property. It is increased by any improvements that you make and decreased by any depreciation and casualty losses taken. Thus, if you sell your home for more than your basis, you have a gain. If you sell your home for less than your basis, you have a loss, which normally wouldn't be deductible for principal residences but is deductible for investment property. The key then is to have as high a basis as possible.

Strategy: Keep a separate folder for all improvements made. I have a folder that holds all improvement receipts and has a sheet that shows check number, who the payee was, date of improvement, nature of the improvement such as new roof or burglar alarm, and so on.

Strategy: Know what increases basis; *Real Estate Tax Secrets of the Rich* includes a chart that shows what items increase basis in Chapter 4. Generally, anything that is new and increases the value of your home is deemed an improvement that increases basis rather than a repair, which has no effect on basis. Examples of improvements would be new door, new skylight, new cable jacks, new roof, new wall, new breakfast room, and so on.

MONEY SAVER:

One of the most overlooked items for basis increases are things that help your property. Thus, every time you pay for new seed and fertilizer, new permanent shrubbery, it increase your basis. I should note that with principal residences, you want improvements over repairs because improvements increase your basis. Repairs are not deductible and also don't increase basis. *Yuck*! However, if you own investment property, you want to try to clarify your expenditures to be repairs because repairs are deductible on investment property.

Strategy: Combine an improvement with a repair. IRS regulations note that if you combine an improvement with a repair as part of one job and one bill, you can treat the whole thing as an improvement.

Example: Your gutters need cleaning. If you simply hire someone to clean out your gutters, it would be a nondeductible repair. If, however, you get a new roof as well as cleaning out the gutters, and get one bill for the whole job, the entire amount paid will be deemed an improvement. Pretty neat, huh?

Piper: How do you keep good records for your taxes?

Botkin: As I noted above, keep a separate file for each property that you own showing all improvements. You want to also keep your settlement sheets, closing papers, improvement receipts, and proof of payment and receipts for all appliances. You might be asking, "Why keep receipts for appliances such as refrigerators?" If any of the appliances transfer as part of the sale of your property, you can add the cost of these appliances to your basis. Many times washers, dryers, dishwashers, furnaces, hot water heaters, built in cabinets, and refrigerators can transfer with the property.

Piper: What is your special tax advice for inheriting property, divorce with property involved, or military?

Botkin: With *inheritance*, you get to "bake your cake and eat it too." If you inherit property, your basis is the fair market value as of the date of death. It is *not* the basis of the property from who you inherited the property. Thus, if your surviving parent paid $300,000 for a home that was worth $1,000,000 at their death, your basis is $1,000,000. Also, there is no gain to the parents and no gain to you! How great is that? Sadly, someone has to die; thus, this isn't my favorite tax-planning strategy.

I should note that in 2010, the estate tax is scheduled to be eliminated. Should this occur and should you inherit property during that year, your basis will not be the fair market value but will be the basis of the property of the deceased. This is another congressional gotcha. Thus, in 2009, I would ask your parents where their settlement papers are located for any real estate or other property that they own.

There is, however, one *huge* trap that everyone who gets *divorced* should know about. Normally, when you buy a home, your initial basis is what you paid. Thus, if you pay $1,000.000 for a home, your basis is $1,000,000. This is, however, not true if you buy out your spouse's interest pursuant to a divorce. If you buy out a spouse pursuant to a divorce, the selling spouse pays no tax on the money given them. This part is great for them.

The buying spouse, however, gets shafted. They get no benefit from the cash given the selling spouse. The buying spouse's basis is the same basis that they had when they first bought the house. Let's use an example to explain this:

Sam and Sarah are married and bought a home several years ago for $200,000. Assume that they are getting divorced when the house is worth $1,000,000. If Sam sells out his half interest to Sarah for $500,000 pursuant to a divorce, Sam doesn't pay any tax on the $500,000 that he received for his interest. Sarah, unfortunately, gets no benefit for the $500,000 paid Sam. Sarah's basis remains her original basis of the home prior to the divorce, which is $200,000.

Strategy: If you are getting a divorce, it is almost always better to sell the house to a third party. Each spouse could then claim the $250,000 exclusion as long as they owned the house for at least two out of the last five years and resided in the house for two out of the last five years. Of course if you are the selling spouse, it probably pays you to keep this problem a secret.

Military folks get a special benefit. They can elect to suspend the five-year period during the time that either spouse is serving on qualified extended duty as a member of the uniformed services or U.S. Foreign Service, up to a maximum election of 10 years. This means that taxpayers may be able to meet the exclusion even if they didn't meet the test because of their service.

Mary and Cody live in their home for three years. Cody, who is a member of the armed services, gets transferred to California from New York for four years. If they were to sell the home right after his four-year tour of duty, they would be eligible for the $500,000 exclusion. They were able to suspend (not count) the time that

Cody spent away on extended duty. Thus, they are deemed to meet the test.

It almost makes me want to joint the military just for this benefit! See IRS Publication Number 3, "Armed Forces Tax Guide.

Piper: What are the tax benefits of homeownership and home sale tax perks?

Botkin: Home sale perks: Generally, as noted previously, you avoid gain ($500,000 married filing jointly or $250,000 single) on the sale of your principal residence if you owned the home for two out of the last five years and occupied it as such. What is most interesting is that the period of ownership and of residency doesn't have to be the same two out of five years.

Example: Jim and Sue are living in a rented home in year one. In year two, they still live in the home but buy the home from the previous owner. In years three and four , Jim gets transferred, and the couple move's away and convert's the home to a rental. In year five, they sell the home. Do they qualify for the full exclusion? The answer is yes!

Here is the reason: They met the residency test in years one and two, even though they didn't own the home in year one. They met the ownership test in years three and four. Thus, they can use the exclusion.

I should note that IRS waives the occupance and residence test *if* you sold your home because of a hardship. A hardship can be for health reasons, divorce, multiple births, new job, loss of a job, or other hardship.

For example, within one year of buying a home, a policemen moved next door with a police dog that kept barking most of the day and night. The couple moved away shortly thereafter claiming a hardship, which was allowed.

Sandy Botkin CPA, Esq. is a former IRS attorney and trainer of IRS attorneys. He is the principal lecturer for the Tax Reduction Institute of Germantown Maryland. This information was obtained from his new book, *Real Estate Tax Secrets of the Rich* (published by McGraw-Hill) and *Lower Your Taxes:BIG TIME*, also published by McGraw-Hill. You can obtain these books at *Amazon.com*, Barnes and Noble, Borders Books, or by going to Sandy's Website at *www.taxreductioninstitute.com*.

Chapter 15

Taking Care of Your New Home Without Breaking the Bank

Whenever you ask homeowners the first thing they did when they moved in, the list looks a little like this: paint, decorate, yard work. We all know the basics, but what we often don't know are the insider low-cost tips that could save us money in the long-term life of owning our home. So, that's why I turned to Dan Osborn, owner of Upstate Home Inspection Service, who has done countless inspections and has a natural enthusiasm for home care. I asked Dan, "What are inexpensive little things we can do to take care of our homes that will save us money in the long run?" This was his excellent advice, verbatim. Check it out:

➪ **Basements:** "If a house does not have gutters or have gutters that don't have extensions—then the rain water that hits a roof is just poured onto the ground right next to the foundation wall. This water then settles into the ground next to the basement wall and is 'absorbed' by the concrete wall. An extension of five feet or more on the gutter forces the water away from the house. The problem is some people look at having gutters as a great thing. It is, but then the gutter drops all the water on the roof right into one corner of the house. That is worse than not having gutters at all. Because all the water is put into one spot. So, adding extensions onto the gutters that places the water at least five feet away is good. This is all in an effort to avoid a wet basement. "Basements all get wet after awhile and people wonder what they can do to keep the basement dry. Dealing with the water is a good way," says Dan. "A dry basement system can cost $5,000 to $10,000. But if you spend $50 on gutter extensions and a couple hundred dollars on grading the soil up close to the house so that it runs away from the house, then you can help keep the water away from your foundation and avoid that wet basement. Of course, these preventative measures work best if done prior to the basement getting wet."

- **Hot water heaters** "have a life expectancy of 10 years or so. If you flush your unit out every other year you can add years to that 10-year life," says Dan. "Sediment builds up in the base of the hot water heater. This sediment deteriorates the interior lining of the hot water heater. A 30-minute job every other year can add many years to the life of a hot water heater. They cost about $400–$500 to replace."
- **Dryers** that aren't vented properly can cause fires and mold in an enclosed area like a laundry room. Mold can be expensive to remediate. But, spending $25 on the correct connector and vent and then makeing sure it is actually venting outside can save you the $2,000 or more on a mold remediation job, says Dan.

One Last Word

Just remember, one day, you will want to sell your home. People are selling their homes quicker and more frequently than in the past. On a day-to-day basis, keep your home up to par, so when you are ready to sell, the process will be easy for you. Keep in mind, a home with great curb appeal (cut shrubs, well-maintained yard, clean gutters, flowers, and so on) will sell for a higher price than a home without that appeal. For the interior of your home, if you ever

Insiders Insight

Through an inspector's eyes:

When I walk through a house at the beginning of an inspection I use all my senses. I try to smell if there are any funny odors. Mold and gas can be smelled. That damp smell in wet basements is a sure sign of problems. I walked into a re-habed 10-year-old house yesterday and it smelled funny. After an hour inspection we figured out, just by the clues left around, that the dishwasher had failed and flooded the first floor and left two inches of water on the floor that then ran down the basement walls and caused mold on the sub-flooring. This was all tipped off by the odor when we walked in. I feel the floor as I walk around to see how the floor feels, it is solid or soft. Does it kind of give as I walk or is it firm? The same for walking upstairs, you can feel the stairs move if it isn't built right. While I do that I listen for creaks or sounds from the floor boards. If they aren't nailed in right they squeak. Sometimes this is an easy fix, sometimes not. But, you get an idea if it was properly built or not. I look for cracks in the walls around windows or doors. This will tell me if the house is moving or not and I look for moisture signs. Stains on ceilings. Repaired patches on ceilings from roof leaks or from plumbing problems. WATER IS THE ENEMY OF THE HOUSE. Keeping water issues under control is the best surefire way of not having problems. So look for stains and smell for mold. Keep your roof working properly and make sure your basement stays dry and you will be home free."

—Dan Osborn

need a quick pick-me-up, the quickest and most effective tactic is a fresh coat of paint (particularly neutral tones, white, cream, tan) that make a room look cleaner, brighter, and more spacious. De-cluttering, grouping together similar knick-knacks, clearing out excessive furniture and maintaining the upkeep of your home will keep you in a good position for the day when you are ready to sell.

From the moment you pick out your home, always think about the day you resell. You'll be glad you did.

MONEY SAVER:

"Everyone has the best intentions the day they buy the house of all the neat things they are going to do. Then they get busy and before they know it, four years has passed by and they still haven't taken care of the two or three items the home inspector told them about. Yeah, they had the addition put on and they had the landscaper take out some trees. But, did they add the extensions on the gutters....

"NO!" says Dan, who recommends homeowners hiring a House Facks inspector to be their consultant. It's a new program Upstate Home Inspection Service has started.

"The House Facks inspector will get to know your house and come back every year and check on all these small things that never get done. He will have a list of trusted local tradesmen that can do the work in a timely manner," Dan says. "The homeowner will save the yearly cost of the program by having the consultant recommend contractors that won't rip off the unsuspecting homeowner. Plus, the homeowner has an ongoing history of the house for insurance purposes. For the day they sell the house, it will be in perfect shape and won't have any surprises or problems at the time of sale.

"Once the inspector knows your house and he calls you up to set up your yearly check-up, he will remind you about the couple of items that are left to be done and he will arrange to have them done. That is what the homeowner needs, someone that he trusts that will advise him about his biggest (appreciating) asset." Visit *www.upstateinspection.com* for more on House Facks or see if an inspector in your area has a similar program.

Chapter 16

Home-Selling Guide

Do you want to sell your home?

It's all about preparing before you put the "For Sale" sign in the yard. It's about knowing how much you want to get for your house (the most you want to get and the least you will take for it), it's about knowing what your profit will be after all the expenses (we have a list of expenses to expect), and, most importantly, it's about preparing your house for the market so it sells. A home with good curb appeal and nice interior tends to sell faster (and for a higher price) than a home without those characteristics.

As soon as your home hits the market, that's when it is hottest—so, first impressions are important. Take the time to improve your home's appeal before hastily putting it on the market. We will cover how to prep your home, price it, find a good Realtor, wrire and place ads that sell, and more.

Preparing Your House for Market

The first step before all else is preparing your house for sale. You can do this before or after finding a Realtor. Following is a handy checklist to help you get your home in shipshape:

☑ Make your home look ready to move in: Fresh paint, clean, declutter, deepclean carpets, and stash away personal photos, degrees, trophies (help the buyer envision living in your home).

- ☑ Show off your square footage: Take up to 2/3 of the furniture out of the rooms. Mirrors help extend a space. Clear out your garage, attic, and shed to show off storage.
- ☑ Great curb appeal = more money: Cut grass, mulch flower beds, trim shrubs, weed, rake leaves, and add flowers/plants to create a welcome appearance.
- ☑ Lighting: Open blinds and turn on lights to create a bright, clean, cheerful appearance.
- ☑ Check your title: Clear/fix any liens against it before selling so this problem doesn't come up later and potentially delay your closing.
- ☑ Pre-inspection: A home inspection before selling your home gives you a chance to make repairs early on or let the buyer know of problems up front. (This is optional. Many times buyers will do their own inspection.)
- ☑ Disclosure: Many states require sellers to make buyers aware of problems with the home or issues that could affect a buyer's decision to buy it. Check with your Realtor or attorney to find out about disclosure/disclaimer laws in your area.

Finding a Realtor

You will want a Realtor that is really looking out for your needs, is very familiar with homes in your area, and is good at sales. Ask for recommendations, notice the Realtor with tons of "For Sale" signs in your area (a sign they know the area well), and, most of all, interview several Realtors before you select one to work with you.

This is what you should genuinely expect from your Realtor. That Realtor should really have a marketing plan when they meet with you for the first time, hoping to get your business. How are they going to sell your home and work for you? Ask them what their plan is. A good Realtor is prepared and has a plan from the moment they meet you.

Hot Tip:

What services should a Realtor offer you?

"First and foremost: honesty and integrity, then a well-thought-out marketing plan, specific to the individual needs of the client, whether buyer or seller. On the listing side, the marketing plan should provide a comprehensive overview of the entire process including brochures, visual tours, advertising, and Web presence. On the buyers side, it is critical to help them find a lender who can create guidelines specific to their financial means. Setting buyers up on the Website for instant access to all the new listings that fit their search criteria will be extremely helpful to them in order to narrow down their search."

—Linda O'Donnell, RE/MAX Signature

Another option is discount brokerages (they sell your home, charging your a discounted price). Some offer an a la carte menu of offerings, such as posting your home on the MLS, taking care of the paperwork, and so on. Among the well-known discount brokerages are *www.assist2sell.com* and *www.helpusell.com.* There are also flat-fee listings (google "flat-fee listing"), with which you pay a fee just to have your home posted on the Multiple Listing Service (a listing of homes for sale) and often times, a buyer's Realtor will call to see if they can show their client your home (and most buyer's agents ask if you will pay their commission). In many of those instances, you would pay one commission for the buyer's agent.

Which leads us to another option, selling as a "for sale by owner." If you do opt to try this route, I really recommend picking up *The For Sale By Owner Handbook* by yours truly.

1. Get 20 directional gound signs (post it at every entrance of your neighborhood and main roadways, watching for area road restrictions), advertising your home is for sale.

2. Put your home on the MLS using a reputable flat-fee listing service (or those grocery-store home sale FSBO magazines that also offer to post your home on the MLS).
3. You may have to offer a buyer's agent a standard commission. (The upside? You won't have to pay a selling agent because you're handling it.)
4. Get a real estate attorney to help with the contract when you find a buyer, if needed.
5. Have a good relationship with a mortgage person, so, if you get any potential buyers who don't know how much they qualify for to buy a home, you have someone to recommend to get the ball rolling.
6. Always have an informational flier attached to a clean appealing sign in your front yard; you can find those fancy wooden-post signs, too. But, make sure your flier includes the basics: price, address, amenities, details about the home, and your contact information.
7. Remember your safety when showing your home.

8. Make sure you really research the going prices in your area to make sure your home is priced properly; get a comparable market analysis from at least three Realtors.
9. Hold open houses, place ads in the paper, and see if you can post your home ad online for free.
10. Enjoy the selling process, know what, you want and don't settle for less.

Pricing Your Home to Sell

Here is the importance of a good Realtor. A good Realtor will pull an accurate comparable market analysis telling you what the price of homes are going for in your area, so it helps you price your home. When you look at the comparable market analysis, also pay attention to the following:

- How long did it take other homes in your area to sell? Was it several weeks or was it months? Then you get a ballpark idea of how long it will take you to sell your home.
- Pay attention to the price sellers asked for and compare it to the actual price their home sold for.
- You will get a feel for whether it is a buyer's market (where there are more home's for sale, which tend to stay on the market longer because of fewer buyers, so the ball is in the buyer's court) or a seller's market (where homes tend to spend little time on the market, sellers typically get close to or asking price, if not higher, and in some cases, multiple offers, where there is smaller pool of homes for sale and many buyers).

Other ways to get a feel for the market, is to do your own grassroots research, too. Browse the paper and visit *www.Realtor.com* to see how much homes are selling for in your area. You can also visit the county assessor's office to see what price homes sold for (many have this online now).

Marketing Plan

If you're working with a Realtor, they will have a marketing plan for you. But, the most important marketing is having your home on the Multiple Listing Service. The other marketing includes the typical open houses, showings, for sale signs, fliers (attached to your sign), online marketing, and newspaper ads. We have some tips for your newspaper ad, it's the hook. Location, price, size, and contact information are the essentials. Now, sell them on the details. The beautiful landscape, irresistible wet bar, and eat-in kitchen. Let them in and make your buyer want more. Following are cost-effective tips for your newspaper ad:

- Abbreviations: Request the newspaper to abbreviate the words in your ad. They will know what abbreviations are common for your area.

- Sales-Packages: Ask about sales packages if you are planning on running more than one ad.
- Internet: Ask the newspaper if they will also post your home on their Website without any additional cost. (Many will.)

- Stand out, cost less: To make your ad stand out, ask the newspaper to do some words in bold, italics, *stars,* or other features that don't cost a lot.

Short Ads	Long Ads
Pros: It's inexpensive. You answer a buyer's up front questions if your ad says: location, price, size, and contact information. You give just enough to spark interest in seeing your home. Cons: You don't share what sets your home apart from others.	Pros: Long ads give you a chance to share what makes your home unique. You tell the buyer about the lush wooded backyard overlooking the lake, the high ceilings, Victorian architecture, and wet bar. You sell it with soul. If an ad doesn't have enough info, you get a lot of calls asking for more info and more visitors. Cons: Newspaper ads cost an arm and a leg.

- Photos: If you add a photo to your ad, it will cost you. But, if you want to add it, go for it. A lot of times you can request the paper to take a photo of your home for the ad at no extra cost to you. Ask your paper.
- Picture perfect: Taking great pictures of your home for ads, fliers, and Websites.

Checklist for the Seller

☑ Price your home right. Look at CMAs from your Realtor or online. Also, check out *Zillow.com*. Get an idea of how much homes are selling for, how long it's taking to sell, and the going price for price per square foot. Visit homes for sale, look online, look at the newspaper. A good equation for pricing your home is the price per square foot x your square footage = sales price.

☑ Preparing for market. Make your home look as good as possible inside and out. A good fresh coat of paint, declutter, clear out excessive furniture, cut the shrubs, maintain the grass, and add flowers for a warm appeal. A home with appealing looks will sell better and for a higher price than a home that is not maintained.

☑ Advertising that works. A good Realtor will have a good marketing plan that has a track record of working with previous clients. He or she will typically place (and pay) to advertise your home in the newspaper, hold open houses, schedule showings, place your home on the multiple listing service, send out fliers, and post signs (and directional signs). A Realtor who is tech-savvy will make sure your home has a good marketing presence online (virtual tours, appealing pictures on online ads, and so on). Ask your Realtor what the marketing plan is for your home and make sure they follow through. Many times, a

Realtor will ask you to sign an agreement that says they are your Realtor for x-number of days/months.

- ☑  Scoring buyers and closing the deal. When buyers present offers, make sure they are pre-qualified (preferably pre-approved) for a loan, which shows they can afford your home. If they give an earnest money deposit and down payment, they are ready to roll. Always let the buyers know what defects are a problem with your home—disclose everything. It is better to be up front than to hide anything. You have a fully executed contract when everything is signed, dated, and agreed upon. Many times buyers request home warranties, so be prepared for that. And the deal is usually contingent on a whole house inspection (and any other inspections specified) and the buyer's ability to attain financing for the home.
- ☑ Steps to closing. After you have a fully executed contract, the buyer will take care of financing and setting up the home inspection, plus any additional inspections.

You will negotiate and take care of repairs after the inspection(s). The seller typically sets up the termite inspection. Call the title company, escrow company, and lawyer or attorney specializing in real estate to take care of your closing. Before closing, the buyer will have a final walk-through of the home to make sure the home is in the same condition or better than when the deal was signed (and to make sure all the repairs, if needed, were made after the inspections). On closing day, you get paid, the buyer gets the keys, and then it gets recorded at the local government office. Congratulations!

Chapter 17

Quick Go-to References for Shoestring Success

Are you considering investing in real estate? This section is meant to be a guide of resources to help you if you are considering investing in real estate.

Books

The following is a list of helpful real estate investment books. While not a complete list, it's one to get you started.

The Beginner's Guide to Real Estate Investing by Gary W. Eldred, PhD (John Wiley & Sons, 2004). Eldred shares techniques for investing in real estate and how to avoid common mistakes.

Investing in Real Estate, 5th Edition by Andrew James McLean and Gary W. Eldred (Wiley; 5th Edition, 2005). A best-selling guide to investing, it features tips on negotiating deals, analyzing market trends, using the Internet as a tool, and how to invest in homes, as well as small apartment buildings.

Real Estate Investing for Dummies by Eric Tyson and Robert S. Griswold (For Dummies, 2004). This book covers investing in single-family homes, condos, vacation homes, apartments, commercial properties, land, and real estate investment trusts.

Rich Dad's Advisors: The ABC's of Real Estate Investing: The Secrets of Finding Hidden Profits Most Investors Miss (Rich Dad's Advisors) by Ken McElroy (Warner Business Books, 2004). Also available is *Rich Dad's Guide to Investing: What the Rich Invest in,*

That the Poor and Middle Class Do Not! by Robert T. Kiyosaki. (Warner Business Books, 2000).

The No-Nonsense Real Estate Investor's Kit: How You Can Double Your Income by Investing in Real Estate on a Part-Time Basis by Thomas Lucier (Wiley, 2006). This book is a step-by-step practical guide for beginners and advanced investors, featuring tips limiting your risk and liability, setting up a real estate business, following state/federal statutes, negotiating deals, and more.

The Wall Street Journal Complete Real Estate Investing Guidebook by David Crook (Three Rivers Press, 2006). This features tax breaks for investors, tips for being a landlord, tips for finding great properties, financing advice, and more.

What Every Real Estate Investor Needs to Know about Cash Flow ...And 36 Other Key Financial Measures by Frank Gallinelli (McGraw-Hill, 2003). This book focuses on calculating cash flow long term, net operating income, financial formulas, and more.

Investing in Duplexes, Triplexes, and Quads: The Fastest and Safest Way to Real Estate Wealth by Larry B. Loftis (Kaplan Business, 2006). This features tips for getting new investors into the game and advice for experienced investors, too.

What No One Ever Tells You About Investing in Real Estate: Real-Life Advice from 101 Success Investors (What No One Ever Tells You About Investing in Real Estate) by Robert J. Hill and Robert Shemin (Kaplan Business, 2004).

Building Wealth One House at a Time: Making it Big on Little Deals by John W. Schaub (McGraw Hill, 2004). Impressively praised by real estate columnist Robert Bruss, who says this is a must-read for serious investors.

Great Big Book on Real Estate Investing: Everything You Need to Know to Create Wealth Real Estate by Stuart LeLand Rider (Entrepreneur Press, 2005). How to find the best properties, how to get into it, and get a CD-ROM with customizable forms and spreadsheets for your finances, return on investment, among other great features.

How to Get Started in Real Estate Investing by Robert Irwin (McGraw-Hill, 2002). This is a book for investors with little or no experience. It gives you the ins and outs to be aware of when investing in real estate.

Website Resources

Following are some great Websites to help you get more information on the topic:

National Real Estate Investor
http://nreionline.com
This site has really great articles on different types of investing, technology, strategies, finances, resources, commentaries, and more.

National Real Estate Investors Association
www.nationalreia.com
A non-profit trade association service the real estate investing industry.

Creative Real Estate Online
www.creonline.com
How-to articles, money ideas, real estate law, financing, books, courses, and more.

Bigger Pockets
www.BiggerPockets.com
Created to help beginner and advanced investors. They say the goal of their site is to teach you about purchasing foreclosures, landlording, rehabbing, wholesaling, land investing, creative financing, commercial and residential real estate investing, and more. It features real estate tools such as: credit reports, find house values (free), maps, mortgage/loan search, and a free rental property analysis tool.

National Association of Real Estate Investment Trusts
www.nareit.com
Many states have real estate investor (or real estate investment trusts) Websites. Just "Google" your state's name and real estate investor and/or real estate investment trusts.

Help for the Home-Buying Process

Here is a list of sources to help you through your home-buying experience. Contacts, resources, Websites, and phone numbers are just a call or click away.

First-Time Homeowner Programs

If you are a first-time homeowner, you can contact your local state housing authority or visit *www.hud.gov/local/index.cfm* for a listing of programs for each state.

Credit Information

Credit is one of the most important parts of buying a new home. Meet with a mortgage officer to check your credit standing and ability to buy. A mortgage officer will be able to help you to improve your credit. To check your credit or learn more about it, these are really great resources:

Free Credit Help Session

Do you need help with your credit situation?
Readers of *Buying Your House on a Shoestring* can have a free credit help session with RMCN Credit Services, Inc.Call: Allen Humphris, General Sales Manager at (972) 529-0900, ext. 251.
E-mail: *a.humphris@rmcninc.com.*

Annual Credit Report

You can request a free credit report from each of the credit reporting agencies—Experian, Equifax, and TransUnion—from *www.annualcreditreport.com.*
P.O. Box 105281 Atlanta, GA 30348-5281
Phone: (877) 322-8228.
Contact information for each of the credit report agencies

TransUnion
P.O. Box 10581 Atlanta, GA

Equifax
P.O. Box 740241 Atlanta, GA 30374
Phone: (800) 685-1111
Website: *www.equifax.com*

Experian

National Consumer Assistance Center

P.O. Box 2104 Allen, TX 75013

Phone: (888) 397-3742

Website: *www.experian.com*

You can also send your credit questions to Maxine Sweet, vice president of public education at Experian, at *www.experian.com/ask_max*.

Fannie Mae

Consumer Resource Center provides a listing of Fannie Mae approved lenders and answers consumer inquiries.

Phone: (800) 732-6643 Website: *www.fanniemae.com*

Federal Citizen Information Center

Check out credit tips on this site. This site also has information on housing, family, education, and computers, just to name a few.

Website: *www.pueblo.gsa.gov*

Phone: (888) 8-PUEBLO (1-888-878-3256)

Federal Trade Commission, Consumer Response Center

You can get free brochures about credit.

6th and Pennsylvania Avenue NW Washington, D.C., 20580

Phone: (877) FTC-HELP

Website: *www.ftc.gov/credit*

First Gov for Consumers

Banking, credit, identity theft, consumer protection, and more.

Website: *www.consumer.gov/yourmoney.htm*

MyFICO.com

Here you can get a lot of credit information and a composite score.

Phone: (800) 319-4433 Website: *www.myfico.com*

National Foundation Credit Counseling

Nonprofit organization offering a program to help improve your credit.

801 Roeder Road, Suite 900, Silver Spring, Maryland, 20910

Phone (800) 388-2227

Website: *www.debtadvice.com*.

TransUnion, LLC
Consumer Disclosure Center
P.O. Box 1000 Chester, PA 19022
Phone: (800) 888-4213
Website: *www.transunion.com*

Pre-Qualified or Pre-Approved

QuickenLoans

If you would like to get pre-approved or pre-qualified, we partnered with Quicken Loans to help you. Quicken Loans is offering a special Website *www.quickenloans.com/shoestring,* or call 800-962-1644, just for readers of *Buying a House on a Shoestring*, who are seeking an asset-verified mortgage approval.

WellsFargo

We also partnered with Wells Fargo to help you, too. Visit Chapter 2 to for the easy-to-fill-out form or visit *www.wellsfargo.com*.

Find a Realtor

Realtor.com To find a real estate agent by city and state, visit National Association of Realtors Website at *www.realtor.com*. This is also a fantastic site for finding homes in your area. Several other great ideas for finding Realtors, visit Websites of local real estate offices in your area. Many of these Websites have agent bios and contact information, so you can learn more about an agent before you interview them. Or visit your local newspaper's Website (or pick up a local paper) and check out the real estate agent ads available; most of the time, they will link to their individual Realtor site to learn more about them. And recommendations from friends, family, and others is always a great stepping stone. Interview several Realtors before selecting one and always see their testimonials and check their references. (Side note: There is a trend in Realtors writing blogs on their Websites. It's interesting reading and you get to know what they are like; you get an idea of their personality and if you would want to work with them.)

Home Inspections

American Society of Home Inspectors, Inc. (ASHI)
932 Lee Street, Suite 101, Des Plaines, Illinois, 60016
Website: *www.ashi.org*
Phone: 1-800-743-ASHI (2744).

National Association of Certified Home Inspectors (NACHI)
1750 30th Street, Boulder, CO 80301
Website: *www.nachi.org*
E-mail: FastReply@nachi.org.

National Association of Home Inspectors, Inc. (NAHI)
4248 Park Glen Road, Minneapolis, MN 55416
Website: *www.nahi.org*
Phone: (952) 928-4641 or (800) 448-3942
Fax: (952) 929-1318
E-mail: info@nahi.org.

Inspector Locator
If you want a particular inspection such as mold or termite, visit *www.InspectorLocator.com*.

USInspect.com
This is a great site for practically every type of inspection (mold, radon, roof,whole-house inspections, and so on.) and sample inspection reports.
Website: *www.usinspect.com*

Tax Perks

Internal Revenue Service:
For more information about tax perks when you buy your home (as well as when you move).
Website:*www.irs.gov.*

Free Guides

Fannie Mae Foundation
The Fannie Mae Foundation has three free guides available to the public. You can get the guides by calling (800) 688-HOME or request it online at *www.fanniemaefoundation.com*:

- Opening the door to a home of your own.
- Choosing the mortgage that's right for you.
- Knowing and understanding your credit.

Mymoney.gov

Federal government's site for investing, saving, and managing money. You can order online at *www.mymoney.gov* the free My Money Tool Kit.

Mortgage and Real Estate Contract Glossary

We asked Jeffrey P. Zane, P.A., for advice. Following, the president of the Attorneys' Real Estate Council of Palm Beach County, Inc., Florida, shares with us real estate contract terms and definitions we should know:

Effective Date: The date that the last of the parties to the contract sign the document. It is important because it is from that date that all of the calculations for timely compliance with the contract's terms are calculated. An example of this is that the financing application must be submitted within five (5) days after effective date.

Financing Contingency: The inclusion of this clause makes the contract contingent upon the Buyer(s) obtaining approval of a loan. It requires the Buyer(s) to use reasonable diligence to obtain the loan. It further requires the Buyer(s) to timely communicate with the Seller(s) the status of its efforts to obtain the loan. Failure to properly communicate with the Seller may nullify the Buyer(s)'s ability to obtain its deposit back even if the Buyer(s) fail to obtain the financing.

Closing Date: This is the date by which the contract calls for the sale and purchase to take place. It is on that date that the money is transferred to the Seller(s) and the deed and mortgage, if any, are executed by the Seller(s) and the Buyer(s) respectively.

Homeowners or Condominium Disclosure: When the Buyer(s) is purchasing either a single family home in a Homeowners Community or a condominium in a Condominium Community the

Seller(s) must give the Buyer(s) a disclosure that reflects the fees, approvals and/or assessments relating to the association. The Buyer(s) is also given three (3) days to review the Association Documents during which time the Buyer(s) can get their deposit back and terminate the contract without penalty.

Survey: A licensed surveyor reviews the property to determine if the are any encroachments onto the property by an adjacent property owner's improvements. The surveyor would also determine if the improvements being purchased falls onto the adjacent property. It would also determine if there are any setbacks and/or restriction violations. The Buyer(s) are required to obtain a survey if there is a loan involved and should obtain a survey even if it is buying the property for cash.

Deed: This is the document that is recorded in the public records and transfers title of the real estate from the Seller(s) to the Buyer(s).

Bill of Sale: This is the document that is not recorded in the public records, but it effectively transfers the personal property that is included in the sale of the real estate.

Mortgage: This is the document that is recorded in the public records and creates a lien on the real estate to secure the real estate as collateral for the loan.

Prorations: There are periodic payments in real estate such as real estate taxes. That payment covers a time frame of January 1st through December 31st. The cost of that real estate tax is prorated to reflect the portion of the year that the Seller(s) are required to pay and a portion of the year that the Buyer(s) are required to pay. The same calculation would be required if there were association assessments, or rental income, and so on.

Seller Disclosure: This requires the Seller(s) to inform the Buyer(s) of any fact(s) that the Seller(s) knows of that materially affects the value of the property which are not readily observable by the Buyer(s).

1031 Exchange: This refers to a tax-free exchange that may be available to either Seller(s) or Buyer(s) that are involved in an investment or commercial real estate transaction.

Windstorm Insurance: This involves insurance protecting against damage caused by wind typically in conjunction with a hurricane or tornado.

Flood Insurance: This involves insurance protecting against damage caused by water flowing from the ground up and not from the sky down.

Homeowners' Insurance: This involves insurance protecting against damages caused by fire, theft, or negligence involving persons on the property, and so on.

Balance to Close Requirements: As part of the real estate closing the closing agent will inform the parties the amount of money they need to bring to the closing in order to complete the transaction. These moneys need to be delivered to the closing agent no later than the time of the closing. The moneys must either be in the form of a wire transfer received by the closing agent or a locally drawn cashier's or official bank check.

Mortgage Terms

Brad Blackwell, executive vice president and retail national sales manager of Wells Fargo, shares with us mortgage terms we should know:

Escrow fees: These cover the costs of preparing and sending all of documents and funds related to the purchase process.

Title Insurance: This coverage is designed to protect both the borrower and the bank on the chance the seller doesn't actually own the home you're buying.

Property Appraisal: To ensure the property you're buying meets their requirements, the lender will have a third-party appraiser estimate the value of the property.

Property Insurance: Nearly every lender requires you to have homeowner's insurance on the property you're purchasing, and you'll typically need to have the policy in place and prepaid for the first year at the time of closing.

Property Inspections: Both the lender and the property insurance company require inspections to ensure the property is structurally sound and free of problems such as termites, mold, water damage, and so forth.

Property Taxes: If the sellers have prepaid any property taxes on the property, you may have to reimburse them for the pro-rated amount.

Private Mortgage Insurance (PMI): This insurance coverage is typically required by the lender if you have a down payment of less than 20 percent of the purchase price. It provides the lender some protection should you default on the loan and enter foreclosure. Once you hit the 20 percent equity threshold—through paying down the principal balance, and/or appreciation, you can typically have this fee removed by paying for another appraisal on your property that shows you've now got more than 20 percent equity.

For other great glossary of mortgage terms, or advice on predatory lending, visit the U.S. Department of Housing and Urban Development at *www.hud.gov*.

Jndex

A

B

C

W

About the Author

Piper Nichole is an award-winning writer, author of *The For Sale By Owner Handbook* for Career Press. Piper is with Lincoln Financial Media for NBC & CBS affiliates. She is the author of hundreds of articles for the *Richmond Times-Dispatch* and a variety of other newspapers and magazines. She also trained professionally in real estate and has passed the real estate licensing exam. Visit Piper online at www.pipernichole.com or email your home buying and selling questions to *pipernichole@gmail.com.*